VOLUME IV

SEASONS
OF THE
LORD

Bible-centered Devotions on
Silence
and
Remembrance

HARPER JUBILEE BOOKS

HJ 1   WILLIAM BARCLAY: The Life of Jesus for Everyman
HJ 2   ERNEST GORDON: Through the Valley of the Kwai
HJ 3   HELMUT THIELICKE: The Waiting Father
HJ 4   PAUL TOURNIER: The Person Reborn
HJ 5   A. W. TOZER: The Knowledge of the Holy
HJ 6   WALTER TROBISCH: I Loved a Girl
HJ 7   WALTER TROBISCH: I Married You
HJ 8   ELTON TRUEBLOOD: The Humor of Christ
HJ 9   ETHEL WATERS: To Me It's Wonderful
HJ 10   ELEANOR SEARLE WHITNEY: Invitation to Joy
HJ 11   SHERWOOD ELIOT WIRT: Not Me, God
HJ 12   JOHN R. BISAGNO: Love Is Something You Do
HJ 13   INGRID TROBISCH: The Joy of Being a Woman
HJ 14   RICHARD WURMBRAND: Victorious Faith
HJ 15   PAUL TOURNIER: A Doctor's Casebook in the Light of the Bible
HJ 16   ELTON TRUEBLOOD: Your Other Vocation
HJ 17   DIETRICH BONHOEFFER: Life Together
HJ 18   CLARENCE W. HALL: Adventurers for God
HJ 19   HERBERT LOCKYER: Everything Jesus Taught, Volume 1
HJ 20   HERBERT LOCKYER: Everything Jesus Taught, Volume 2
HJ 21   HERBERT LOCKYER: Everything Jesus Taught, Volume 3
HJ 22   HERBERT LOCKYER: Everything Jesus Taught, Volume 4
HJ 23   HERBERT LOCKYER: Everything Jesus Taught, Volume 5
HJ 24   ULRICH SCHAFFER: Love Reaches Out
HJ 25   INGRID TROBISCH: On Our Way Rejoicing!
HJ 26   HELEN WESSEL: The Joy of Natural Childbirth
HJ 27   WILLIAM BARCLAY: Everyday Prayers
HJ 28   PAUL TOURNIER: The Adventure of Living
HJ 29   DAVID A. REDDING: The Parables He Told
HJG 01 WILLIAM BARCLAY: A Life of Christ
HJG 02 HERBERT LOCKYER: Seasons of the Lord, Volume 1
HJG 03 HERBERT LOCKYER: Seasons of the Lord, Volume 2
HJG 04 HERBERT LOCKYER: Seasons of the Lord, Volume 3
HJG 05 HERBERT LOCKYER: Seasons of the Lord, Volume 4

VOLUME IV

SEASONS OF THE LORD

Bible-centered Devotions on

Silence
and
Remembrance

HERBERT LOCKYER

A HARPER JUBILEE GIANT

HARPER & ROW, PUBLISHERS

New York, Hagerstown, San Francisco, London

FIRST EDITION

A HARPER JUBILEE GIANT ORIGINAL

Designed by Eve Kirch Callahan

Library of Congress Cataloging in Publication Data

Lockyer, Herbert.
   Seasons of the Lord.
   (Harper jubilee books; HJG 02-05)
   CONTENTS: v. 1. Bible-centered devotions on purity and hope.—v. 2. Bible-centered devotions on resurrection and glory.—v. 3. Bible-centered devotions on fulfillment and splendor. [etc.]
   1. Bible—Meditations—Collected works.
I. Title.
BS483.5.L6   242'.08   76-9998
ISBN: 0-06-065268-3

77 78 79 80 81 8 7 6 5 4 3 2 1

Contents

Preface   ix

Enchantment

The Survival of Unfittest   2

Sole Daughter of My House and
Heart   3

The Sword and the Trowel   4

If You Have Great Talents,
Industry Will Improve Them   5

Where Jesus Is, 'Tis Heaven
There   6

Solitude Is the Mother Country
of the Strong   8

I Loathe Myself When God I
See   9

In His Good Time   10

Memory, the Bosom-spring of
Joy   12

Great Things Are Done When Men
and Mountains Meet   13

Our Sanctuary of Peace   14

Have Mercy on Us Worms of
Earth   15

Constancy Lives in Realms
Above   17

Beauty, Truth, and Love in Thee
Are One   18

His Word Is His Bond   19

What Light through Yonder
Window Breaks   20

Less Than We Deserve   22

Like—But Oh How Different!   23

Dear to God, Dearer We Cannot
Be   24

Such Things As Were Most
Precious to Me   25

Boundless, Endless, and
Sublime   27

Let Me Hide Myself in Thee   28

Grow Old Along with Me   29

The Sweet Omniscience of
Love   30

Secret and Insidious Perils   32

The Bounds of Freedom Wider
Yet   33

God's Nightingales   34

Perseverance Keeps Honor
Bright   36

Bring Me My Chariot of Fire   37

Sore Let and Hindering in Running
the Race   38

Who Shall Ever Find Joy's
Language?   39

Silence and Remembrance

The Grand Perhaps   42

Trust God: See All, nor Be
Afraid   43

Ingratitude, Thou Marble-hearted
Fiend   44

Thy Sweet Converse and
Love So Deeply
Joined   45

He Has Not Escaped Who Drags
His Chain   46

Faith Shines Equal, Arming Me
from Fear   48

Gladly Would He Learn and
Gladly Teach   49

Ye Are Living Poems   50

No Pains—No Gains   52

Habit Rules the Unreflecting
Herd   53

Tears and Smiles Like Us He
Knew   54

Fine Nets and Stratagems to Catch
  Us In 55
Hark, the Glad Sound! 56
In Confidence Shall Be Your
  Strength 57
Approach My Soul the Mercy
  Seat 59
I Sing the Progress of a Deathless
  Soul 60
My Great Taskmaster's Eye 61
You Told a Lie, an Odious
  Damned Lie 62
The Roots of Sin Are There 63
The Last Enemy Destroyed by
  Emmanuel 65

A Wise and Masterly
  Inactivity 66
Be Famous Then by Wisdom 68
Such Are the Gates of
  Paradise 69
He Did Entreat Me Past All
  Saying Nay 70
Human Nature's Daily Food 71
Shining Ones, Whose Faces Shone
  As the Light 72
Do It and Make Excuses 74
Be Swift in All Obedience 75
Little Things Are Infinitely the
  Most Important 76
A Portion of the Eternal 77

Death Yet Life

My Mind Aspire to Higher
  Things 80
Treasure of Light in Earthen
  Vessels 81
Prayer is the Breath of the
  Soul 82
You May Be Mistaken 83
All Chance-Direction Which Thou
  Canst Not See 84
Dig for Victory 86
An Ancient Timekeeper 87
A Little Boy Who Was King 88
The Polished Corners of the
  Temple 89
A Lot of Little Things 91
What's in a Name? 92
The Liberal Deviseth Liberal
  Things 93
Strives in His Little World of
  Man 94
For His Bounty—There Was No
  Winter In't 96
Out of Debt, Out of Danger 97

Like a Living Coal His Heart
  Was 98
Adversary versus Advocate 99
Clear Shining after Rain 100
His Droppings of Warm
  Tears 102
Every Fool Will Be Meddling 103
Thou Hast Conquered, O
  Galilean 104
The Household of
  Continuance 105
Thought Is the Child of
  Action 107
None of Self, and All of
  Thee 108
Veni, Veni, Emmanuel! 109
Lessons from a Spider's Web 110
Threefold Cord of Gospel
  Truth 111
Brothers All in Honor 113
O Living Waters, Rise within Me
  Evermore 114
The Lamp That Ever Shines 115
To Endless Years the Same 116

Preface

At last, in our odyssey, we come to the final quarter of our circular journey. In October the artist's fingers itch to capture with brush and paint the loveliest colors nature has spilled over woodlands and hills with an enchanting range of shadows. Some years ago the Chicago *Tribune* ran a series of attractive vignettes on the twelve months of the year, each illustrated by drawings, events, and proverbs. For October the paper had a cartoon entitled "I am the month of splendor and enchantment." Can we say that our lives are adorned with the beauty of the Lord?

Like the dog with a bad name, November finds it hard to escape from its gloomy, unhappy tradition—an unfortunate reputation for being a month of chilly winds, dark days, gloom and fog, and gray skies. Yet, while there is less activity in the woodlands because creatures have begun their winter sleep, November often presents an attractive face and can change from smiling severity to caressing gentleness. In November we celebrate Veterans Day, remembering those who died in a useless war. O God! Why do men make wars?

At last we complete the circle, finding ourselves in December. Extremes meet during this month, for it is the deathbed of another life to come. This month reminds us that the Lord of the years and the potentate of time was born that we might not die or live eternally in the morgue of sin. As we leave this final month in which decay is all around, let us ever treasure the fact that God gave us memory that we might have roses in December.

x

ENCHANTMENT

Bright October was come,
the misty-bright October.

—Arthur Hugh Clough,
"The Bothie of
Tober-na-Vnolich VI"

The Survival of Unfittest

"Jonathan hath yet a son, who is lame on his feet."
2 Samuel 9:3.

This chapter revolving around David and Mephibosheth is rich in the virtues of loyalty, kindness, and love. The phrase used by the famed biologist Herbert Spencer, "The survival of the fittest," may appear accurate as we observe the struggle for existence. But often God plans that the unfittest shall survive, that when the strongest, bravest, and chiefest pass away, no one remains alive but a Mephibosheth. Saul and Jonathan had been slain in battle, the latter leaving behind a son who was but five years old.

Long years passed, and David, who reigned undisputed over Israel, remembered the covenant he had made with Jonathan. How could he forget that trysting in the fields! So, inquiring about Saul's family, he asked, "Is there yet any that is left in the house of Saul?" and he discovered the crippled son of his dear friend Jonathan. But David took no notice of Mephibosheth's legs and feet. Generously he received this unfit, remaining member of Saul's family and heaped upon him loving-kindness for his father's sake. Years before, when they were close friends, David pledged that he would care for Jonathan's family if he were slain. True to his vow David blessed Mephibosheth, giving him all that had been his father's.

Throughout 2 Samuel 9 we have the refrain, "For Jonathan's sake," and this kindness for another's sake is a parable of the love of God who blesses and enriches us for the sake of his only begotten Son. Sinners may be spiritually lame, poor, and forgotten, but a greater than David, through his grace, restores a lost inheritance and takes the lost and helpless into a rich fellowship with himself. David was not kind to Mephibosheth because of his severe lameness, but for the sake of Jonathan his father. It is thus that God deals with those crippled by sin. Through matchless grace he restores them for the sake of his Son. It is for his sake that God receives and blesses.

Sole Daughter of My House and Heart

"He had one only daughter, about twelve years of age."
Luke 8:42.

When father and mother knelt beside the bed in the Jewish quarter of Capernaum, they hoped against hope that their only child would be spared. An unnoticed feature of the raising of Jairus' daughter is that she was an *only* daughter, possibly like "Ada, sole daughter of my house and heart," about whom Lord Byron wrote in "Childe Harold." How often *one* thing, *one* person, stands at the center of a Gospel scene or story. The shepherd lost *one* sheep; the woman lost *one* coin; the widow of Nain had but *one* son; and in the grief-stricken home of Jairus was *one* daughter. While it is thrilling to know that around the throne of God in heaven *thousands* of children stand, we magnify him for his personal love and grace. "The Son of God Who loved *me*" (Gal. 2:20). An unknown poet wrote:

Thou art as much His care, as if beside
Nor man nor angel lived in heaven or earth.

When his precious solitary child was at the point of death, at the break of day Jairus sought Jesus and in all humility implored him to spare his daughter. The day before the disciples cried "Master" as shipwreck faced them; *fear for themselves* made them call for help. But when Jairus cried "Master," *love for his only child* forced his plea.

What different impulses lead us to kneel before the compassionate Jesus for aid! Reaching the house of death, Jesus emptied it of those who had rudely invaded it, especially the professional mourners who were paid to weep in death chambers. As the Lord of life, he raised the young maid from the dead. Having perfect sincerity, Jesus hates all shams.

An aspect of the miracle is the unfailing thoughtfulness of Jesus seen in his command that the resurrected child should be given food. Jairus and his wife dearly loved their daughter, but in the joy of that hour of restored life they had not noticed that she was hungry. All spiritual awakening is the work of the Spirit, but because the young are the most easily awakened, let us bring them to Jesus before the grave-clothes bind them.

The Sword and the Trowel

"Everyone with one of his hands wrought in his work, and with the other hand held a weapon." *Nehemiah 4:17*.

Nehemiah, cupbearer to the king of Persia, is conspicuous as one of the godliest and bravest characters in Scripture. The good hand of the Lord was upon him in his honorable position in the palace; he had an easy life and every comfort. But his noble soul was burdened to see Jerusalem in ruins and he surrendered his lucrative sphere to face hardships and peril repairing the walls of the city. A greater than Nehemiah was rich but became poor; he suffered much and died that he might restore sin-ruined humanity.

Nehemiah 4 records the trials and difficulties confronting Nehemiah in his patriotic task. Enemies surrounded him, but slowly and surely the great work was accomplished in the face of much opposition. No true work that is worth the doing is done easily. But while a most practical man, conspicuous for his deeds, Nehemiah was preeminently a man of prayer. Behind the hands holding the sword and the trowel was the beating heart of prayer, which never hinders the highest service. Nehemiah's men were both soldiers and builders. Toiling with their trowels, they held their swords always ready for battle. As they labored, their ears were alert, and at the sound of the trumpet they would muster. Actually their work of building the shattered walls was a warfare in disguise.

What a truth is enshrined in this record for your heart and mine! We are builders, and the wall is rising. Underneath is a sure foundation, but as we build, we have to battle, taking to ourselves the whole armor of God. The trowel of service must be accompanied by the sword of the Spirit, by which we are able to fight the good fight of faith with all our might and, in fellowship with Jesus, assist in the building of his church.

If You Have Great Talents, Industry Will Improve Them

"Lord, thou deliverest unto me five talents, behold, I have gained beside them five talents more." *Matthew 25:20.*

Sir Joshua Reynolds, the famous artist, said in a lecture to the students of the Royal Academy, "If you have great talents, industry will prove them: but if you have but moderate abilities, industry will supply their deficiency." In our Lord's parable of the talents the man with five talents certainly worked hard and doubled their worth. The man with only one talent was of moderate ability yet failed through lack of industry to multiply what he had. One evident lesson of this parable then is, *Use it or lose it.*

The parables of the ten virgins and the ten talents, if not spoken by Jesus at the same time, were likely intentionally placed by Matthew because of the light one throws on the other. The story of the virgins is a parable of *watching*, while that of the talents is a parable of *working*. As watchers Christians are meant to *work*, and as workers they must *watch*. From an unknown source we learn: "The former parable centres in the *heart-supplies*, while the latter story moved in the sphere of *outward service*, indicating that, in the Christian life, the heart must always come before the hand."

The five virgins failed because they were oversanguine and easy; the one-talent man failed because he was overcareful and afraid. A further lesson to be learned from the talents is that our gifts are proportioned to our power of using them. If we are faithful in the least and over a few things, the Lord will make us rulers over many things. It is not enough to have a gift or gifts. They must be used, for God is disappointed when someone not only misuses a talent, but does nothing with it. Shakespeare wrote in *Measure for Measure:*

> *Heaven doth with us as we with torches do;*
> *Not light them for themselves; for if our virtues*
> *Did not go forth of us, 'twere all alike*
> *As if we had them not.*

5

Where Jesus Is, 'Tis Heaven There

"Lord, it is good for us to be here." Matthew 17:4.

When Luke gave his report of the transformation, he said that Peter was dazed and dazzled by the outflashing of our Lord's inherent glory and by the appearance of the glorified saints, Moses and Elijah. "Not knowing what he said," Peter voiced, not only his delight at being in such august company, but also his desire to build three tabernacles for the three distinguished ones and stay forever on the mount. Peter erred in retaining the three in association—Moses, the lawgiver; Elijah, the prophet-reformer; Jesus, the promised Messiah. Jesus is not to be looked upon as one among others. When the Master is present, servants must go. So when Peter opened his eyes, he saw "Jesus only" and in so many ways confessed, in the words of Charles Wesley, "Thou, O Christ, art all I want!"

It is, of course, spiritually beneficial to be in the presence of Jesus, living and walking in fellowship with him; and it is good to be numbered with God's people, witnessing with them in a world of sin. But there are other significant applications that can be made concerning this narrative. Peter expressed pleasure when he said, "It is good to be here." When we come to the trials and burdens of life or to a bed of affliction, can we say, "Lord, it is good to be here"? Do we honor him by our loving submission and patient suffering? In our daily task, no matter what our occupation as long as it is legitimate, do we say, "Lord, it is good to be here, for I have opportunities of manifesting forbearance and testifying to thy matchless grace and power"?

If we are truly the Lord's, it is always good to be anywhere, to do anything, as long as he is being glorified by our witness. If our chief aim is to honor him, then no matter where we are, our hearts will say, "Lord, it is good to be here!" Once we reach heaven, from which Moses and Elijah traveled down to the mount, and find ourselves in their company and among the redeemed of all ages and, above all, with our glorified Savior, then with perfect delight we will say, "Lord, it is good to be *here!*"

Solitude Is the Mother Country of the Strong

"Jesus went into the Mount of Olives." John 8:1.

This mount holds a unique place in the awe and affection of those who love and follow Jesus, for it was the scene of his periodical solitude, a habitual haunt of his when he detached himself from the crowds to be alone with God. When day was over, everyone went home, but Jesus, with no home of his own, went to the Mount of Olives to be alone and pray. With the daily pressure of preaching, teaching, and miracle-working, at times Jesus "had not leisure so much as to eat" (Mark 6:31), and his season of solitude preserved the poise and power in his life. Even Jesus could not live continually in the limelight.

Poets have ever praised the virtue of solitude. Edward FitzGerald could say, "The thoughtful soul to solitude retires." John Milton wrote in *Comus:*

> *. . . And Wisdom's self*
> *Oft seeks to sweet retired solitude,*
> *Where with her best nurse Contemplation*
> *She plumes her feathers, and lets grow her wings,*
> *That in the various bustle of resort*
> *Were all too ruffled, and sometimes impair'd.*

Milton also reminded us that "solitude sometimes is best society." Shelley confessed, "I love tranquil solitude"; and Wordsworth wrote in "A Poet's Epitaph," "Impulses of deeper birth, have come to him in solitude." He also described "the self-sufficing power of solitude."

We sing that "faith has still its Olivet and love its Galilee." Galilee shared with Olivet the honor of being a habitual resort of Jesus. Has your faith an Olivet and a Galilee? Have you learned that seasons of solitude are the sanity and sanctity of your life and living, that periods of retirement to be alone with God and his word are an imperative necessity? If so, at all cost keep these sacred trysts with him on *your* mount, no matter where it is.

I Loathe Myself When God I See

"Though I be nothing." *2 Corinthians 12:11.*

Self-depreciation is not attractive to those of the world. Instead of singing, "O to be nothing, nothing," they repeat the refrain, "O to be something, something." The philosophy of humanism exalts individuals by telling them that they are all-sufficient in themselves to achieve what they desire. The humanist despises the virtue of self-abnegation and rejects the Pauline doctrine that no good thing dwells in the flesh. Carlyle could write of "the golden-calf of Self-love—the idol of all lovers of self-worship."

Without doubt the greatest figure in New Testament history after Jesus is Paul, who never thought too highly of himself. He wrote, "Though I be nothing" (2 Cor. 12:11); "the least of all saints" (Eph. 3:8); "the chief of sinners" (1 Tim. 1:15); "in me dwelleth no good thing" (Rom. 7:18). The apostle was blissfully content in exalting the Master he dearly loved and sacrificially served. The more he knew and saw of himself, the more humbled in dust before a thrice-holy God he became. The person outside of Christ will and *must* be something, but the lower the Christian falls before God, the happier and holier will be the outcome. The Christian is willing to be nothing that Christ may be everything, for apart from Christ the Christian is less than nothing.

All we are in grace is *by* Christ; all we have is *from* Christ; all we shall be is *through* Christ. We are empty, but he fills us, we are lost and ruined by the Fall, but he saves us; we are naked, but he clothes us; we are helpless, but he strengthens and sustains us. May we be delivered from fancying we deserve more than we receive, either from God or from others. Let us sing with E. E. Hewitt:

> *Lower and lower; yet higher we rise,*
> *Lifted in Jesus, led on to the skies;*
> *Humbly we follow the way of the Cross,*
> *Then, crowns of glory, and gains for all loss.*

In His Good Time

"I called him, but he gave me no answer."
Song of Solomon 5:6.

Shakespeare wrote in *I Henry VI* that "delays have dangerous ends," but this is not so with divine delays, which are ever beneficial since they develop trust and patience in the soul that waits for heaven's response. God's delays in prayer must not be mistaken for denials. Though he tarries, we must wait his good time, for he will surely come to our aid. There are times when needs are pressing and help is urgent but our prayers seem to rebound in our ears as from a brazen sky. God is not deaf or indifferent to our cry, but often when he gives great faith, he tests it by long delays. We may have felt like Jeremiah who said of the God who hears and answers in his good time, "Thou covereth thyself with a cloud, that our prayer should not pass through" (Lam. 3:44).

But all prayers, inspired by the Spirit and offered by sincere hearts, *always* get through and, although not answered immediately, are not unheard. As Charles H. Spurgeon said:

> God keeps a file for our prayers—they are not blown
> away by the wind, they are treasured up in the King's
> archives. This is a registry in the Court of Heaven wherein
> every prayer is recorded. Tried believer, thy Lord hath
> a tear-bottle in which the costly drops of sacred grief are
> put away, and a book in which thy holy groanings are
> numbered. By-and-by, thy suit shall prevail . . . . God's
> long-dated bills will be punctually honoured; we must
> not suffer Satan to shake our confidence in the god of truth
> by pointing to our unanswered prayers.

Fellow believer, are your prayers for the salvation of dear ones unanswered yet? Then do not mistake delay for denial. God is the sovereign Lord who gives according to his own good pleasure. If he is exercising your patience by not opening his gate at once, remember that he can do as he wills with his own. Rest assured, he will answer "in his good time."

Memory, the Bosom-spring of Joy

"This I recall to my mind, therefore have I hope."
Lamentations 3:21.

A Cockney boy when asked, "What is memory?" quickly replied, "The fing yer fogets wiv." Shakespeare's Lady Macbeth says that memory is "the warder of the brain." Memory is not only "the bosom-spring of joy," as Coleridge called it; it is likewise the bosom-spring of eternal anguish, for the rich man in hell found that memory would be part of the flame tormenting him. "Son, remember . . . thou art tormented" (Luke 16:25). Tennyson said that the truth the poet sings is, "That a sorrow's crown of sorrow is remembering happier things."

In his third lamentation Jeremiah recalled that the Lord's mercy and compassion had not failed him through all past affliction and misery, and this stimulated his hope and trust in his compassionate Lord. Memory can become the bondslave of despondency if the mind feeds on the dark foreboding of past sin. But although Jeremiah called to remembrance the cup of mingled gall and wormwood of former days, he transformed the cup into comfort. "Therefore have I hope" (Lam. 3:21). Like a two-edged sword, the prophet's memory first killed his pride and then slew his despair. An unknown author wrote:

> As a general principle, if we would exercise our memories
> more wisely, we might, in our very darkest distress, strike
> a match which would instantaneously kindle the lamp of
> comfort. Memory need not wear a crown of iron, she may
> encircle her brow with a fillet of gold, all spangled
> with stars.

The seventeenth-century poet Henry Vaughan wrote:

> *They are all gone into the world of light,*
> *And I alone sit lingering here;*
> *Their very memory is fair and bright,*
> *And my sad thoughts doth clear.*

Great Things Are Done When Men and Mountains Meet

"Get thee up into the high mountain." *Isaiah 40:9*.

The history of Bible mountains confirms these lines of William Blake:

> *Great things are done when men and mountains meet;*
> *This is not done by jostling in the street.*

In the introduction to his book *Peaks and Glaciers* E. H. Blakeney remarked "In all times and among all people the mystery and majesty of the hills have, it may be unconsciously, exercised some benignant influence; there is something in their preternatural calm, their august purity, and their solitude that, while humbling the earth-bound spirit, at the same time lifts it nearer Heaven whence it came." The Vulgate version of Psalm 84:5 reads, "Blessed is the man who, nerved by Thee, hath set his heart on ascents."

Since there is a certain security of elevation about divine purity and goodness, Isaiah called upon Zion to get up into the high mountain. "Thy righteousness is like the great mountains" (Ps. 36:6). Ancient Greeks regarded the hills as the home of the gods. The native name for the crests around Mt. Everest was *Diva Dlunga*—God's seat. We can understand, then, how saints of old lifted up their eyes unto the hills to learn their mystic secret. The higher one climbs some hills, the more one is thrilled with the widening prospect.

Is this not so in spiritual experience? The higher we climb, the clearer view we have of the glory and beauty of him who called the mountains into being. The peaks of many Bible mountains were the stepping stones of deity upon which God and men met. John Ruskin, a fervent lover of hill-climbing, said, "My most intense happinesses have been amongst the mountains." As Paul neared his end, death seemed like gaining the summit of a mountain from which he could view the whole of the faithfulness and love of Jesus, to whom he had committed his soul. "I know whom I have believed" (2 Tim. 1:12). May we prove the blessedness of those who set their hearts on ascents.

13

Our Sanctuary of Peace

"My people shall dwell in quiet resting places."
Isaiah 32:18.

The unregenerate do not experience peace and rest. Their hearts are like the waters of a troubled sea that cannot rest. Jonah found a resting place beneath his gourd, but it withered away, and the runaway prophet was left without shelter. Jesus himself is the quiet resting place of those redeemed by his precious blood, and in him they are safe and sheltered forever. None and nothing can destroy him who is our shelter. The Revised Version translates our text, "My people shall dwell in a peaceable habitation."

Paul called the body of the believer "the earthly house of this tabernacle" (2 Cor. 5:1), which is the soul's brief and fragile house and which Jesus chooses as his peaceable home until the earthly house perishes. The grave, the body's long and gloomy habitation, was to Job "mine house; I have made my bed in the darkness" (Job 17:13). But this is by no means a peaceable habitation. Its silence is that of death.

There is, however, a sure dwelling place for the soul and the body of the child of God, namely, the blessed and perpetual resting place which Jesus called "My Father's house." No plague can come nigh this dwelling. Within it there is room for the great multitude no one can number of the redeemed, for this peaceable habitation has many mansions. The reality of this eternal sanctuary of rest is confirmed by the affirmation of Jesus, "If it were not so, I would have told you" (John 14:2).

Having lived with the Father through the eternal past, Jesus knew all about its peace. John Bunyan described his longing for heaven thus: "Now, just as the gates were opened to let in the men, I looked in after them, and behold, the city shone like the sun. Which, when I had seen, I wished myself among them." Praise God, someday—it may be sooner than we expect—we shall hear a voice for our eternal happiness say, "Come up hither!" Then shall we be at home with the Lord.

Have Mercy on Us Worms of Earth

"Have mercy upon me, O God." *Psalm 51:1.*

Whether William Carey's epitaph had any influence on the prayer of Frederick W. Faber, "God Most High, have mercy on us worms of earth," we have no means of knowing. When brought low by a dangerous illness, the famous missionary to India was asked, "If this sickness should prove to be fatal, Dr. Carey, what passage would you select as the text for your funeral sermon?"

He replied, "Oh, I feel that such a poor sinful creature is unworthy to have anything said about him; but if a funeral sermon must be preached, let it be from the words, 'Have mercy upon me, O God.'" In the same spirit of humility Carey directed in his will that the following inscription and nothing more should be cut on his gravestone:

WILLIAM CAREY, BORN AUGUST 17th, 1761: DIED
A wretched, poor, and helpless worm
On Thy kind arms I fall.

After his death in 1834 Carey's wish was carried out. "Have mercy upon us miserable sinners" is among the prayers of the Anglican church; and mercy, the sinner's initial and fundamental need, is shown by God to the repentant in virtue of him who bore the load of sin in his own body on the tree and by his death canceled our guilt.

In the Apocrypha we find the confession, "We will fall into the hands of the Lord, and not into the hands of men: for as His majesty is, so is His mercy." Robert Browning wrote, "Mercy every way is Infinite," and this divine attribute of mercy seasons justice. Only on the footing of free grace can the holiest and most honored approach God, and those who seek to serve the Lord best are most conscious of sin within themselves. What a precious gospel it is to preach that inexhaustible mercy waits to be gracious to a world of sinners lost and ruined by the Fall. Would that the cry would rise from millions of stricken hearts today, "God be merciful to me, a sinner!"

Constancy Lives in Realms Above

"As I was . . . I will be." Joshua 1:5.

The truth of divine constancy runs like a golden thread through Scripture. The Lord is conspicuous as the unchanging and unchangeable companion on life's highway. "I am the Lord, I change not" (Mal. 3:6). Joshua was assured that the divine presence and protection vouchsafed to Moses would likewise be his portion as he assumed command of Israel. The courageous leader proved that God unalterably adhered to all his promises. Reiterating the promise repeated to Joshua, the writer to the Hebrews asserted that "Jesus Christ is the same yesterday, today, and forever" (Heb. 13:8). Persons may change, but Jesus never. Glory to his name!

James, writing of God as "the Father of lights" (1:17), affirmed that "in whom there is no variation or changing shadow" (Charles Williams, tr.). Because of all he is in himself, God cannot vary or change between shadow and substance. All God has ever been, he is and will be forevermore. As Jean Ingelow expressed it:

> *The course of God is one. It likes not us*
> *To think of Him as being acquaint with Change;*
> *It were beneath him!*

Said St. Theresa of Avila, "All things are passing! God never changeth."

Ours is the full confidence that God, having been our help in ages past, will continue to be our hope for years to come. His is an unchanging love. As we retrace the path of the past, we bless him because his goodness has never failed, and thus cheerfully we lay our hands in his for the rest of the way, believing that all he has been he will be until we enter his presence above. What a sheet anchor in the storms of life is God's unchangeableness! Earth's joys may grow dim and its glories pass away, but, as Henry F. Lyte learned, faith sings:

> *Change and decay in all around I see;*
> *O Thou who changest not, abide with me.*

Beauty, Truth, and Love in Thee Are One

"Let the beauty of the Lord be on us." Psalm 90:17.

Scripture has much to say about beauty as associated with God, persons, and things. But what exactly is this quality? The dictionary explains beauty as being "a combination of qualities that delights the sight or mind." We connect beauty mainly with the features and form of the body.

Absalom was renowned for his beauty, to which his luxurious hair contributed but which, alas, brought about his death. If only he had been as good as he was beautiful! Doubtless this rebellious son inherited his beauty from his father, for David is described as being of "a beautiful countenance, and goodly to look to" (1 Sam. 16:12). But, as we say, "Beauty is skin deep," and disease or accident can quickly distort a lovely face.

When the Bible speaks about "beholding the beauty of the Lord," it does not imply facial beauty. Since no one has seen God at any time, one cannot describe God's features. Commentaries explain the phrase "the beauty of the Lord" as "the delight of the Lord" or meditation on the graciousness of God. Beauty, Truth and Love in Thee are one, and we are called to worship him in "the beauty of holiness."

Keats said, "Beauty is truth, truth beauty." Certainly God loves beauty, for he created a beautiful world. John Milton spoke of beauty as "Nature's coin" and as "Nature's brag." Dr. A. J. Gossip, unique Scottish preacher of a past decade, loved to tell the story of the great explorer, Mungo Park. After journeying days and miles in the desolate wilds of China, Park quite suddenly saw at his feet a little blue flower and said gently, "God has been here!" Although God made all things bright and beautiful, his beauty he would have us adorn is an inner spiritual beauty. This is his "diadem of beauty" for his people. In Gossip's hymn to intellectual beauty are lines we can lift to a higher source:

> *Spirit of Beauty, Thou canst consecrate*
> *With thine own hues all Thou dost shine upon,*
> *Of human thought or form.*

His Word Is His Bond

"I trust in thy word." Psalm 119:42.

We have different ways of describing those who say one thing and do another or those whose word is not to be relied on: "He's not a man of his word"; "He's a double-dealer, promising one thing, but doing another"; "He never says what he means"; "His deeds contradict his promises." A person can be trusted only when words and actions harmonize. "Suit the action to the word, the word to the action," said Shakespeare in Hamlet, and this is what God always does. He spoke and it was done. Emerson told us that "words and deeds are quite indifferent modes of divine energy. Words are also actions, and actions are a kind of words."

David could trust what God had said because he knew that what God had promised, he was able and would fulfill. Over and over again the psalmist had proved that God would not lie, that not one good word of his would fail, that he was not only in his words most wonderful, but most sure in all his ways.

A promise is God's bond, and he will keep it. Trusting in his word, we set our minds at rest and wait calmly and in confidence for the fulfillment of his promise. Believing that God is as good as his word, we fear no foe, dread no trial, because we know that he will be faithful in undertaking for us as he said he would. Knowing that there must always be a performance of those things the Lord tells us in his Word, we must believe a promise suited to our need, plead it, rely on it, and expect its fulfillment.

If we cannot take God's Word and depend upon it, what can we trust? Our comfort and encouragement is that divine truths have been tried by numberless saints down the ages and have been found faithful. Trusting in God's unalterable Word brought them, as it brings us, peace of mind, joy to the soul, and all that is necessary in time of need.

What Light through Yonder Window Breaks

"Bind this line of scarlet thread in the window."
Joshua 2:18.

A window was the way of escape for the two spies befriended by Rahab. After hiding them at the peril of her life, "she let them down by a cord through the window." The scarlet thread from the same window was to be a true token that, when Joshua invaded Jericho, Rahab and all her relatives would be delivered from death.

What an apt illustration this presents of an alarmed and repentant sinner, saved by grace through promise, relying on the scarlet sign because of the declared Word! Calvary is the scarlet thread in God's window assuring us of safety when his righteous judgments are abroad. John Milton wrote, "At my window bid Good-Morrow," but there can only be a "Good-Morrow" for you if the scarlet thread hangs from the window of your heart. If God does not see his Son's blood upon you and yours, he cannot pass over you.

Doubtless, the same scarlet cord that preserved the spies preserved Rahab and her family. One proviso that the spies made was that no soldier would attack Rahab's house when Jericho was under siege and no relative of hers would be taken captive and killed if he or she were under the token of the scarlet thread. We can imagine with what zest Rahab went round gathering her parents and all their household to bring them with haste to the house of safety. Her own kith and kin were saved from death purely for Rahab's sake. When Joshua finally entered Jericho, light broke through Rahab's window for all who were behind it, with its scarlet token dangling.

Thrice happy are we if all the members of our family are in the house of safety, free from condemnation because they are in Christ Jesus. Can it be that you still have a dear, unsaved loved one? Then by divine grace may you be enabled to bring them behind the shelter of Calvary's scarlet thread before it is too late.

Less Than We Deserve

"I will correct you in measure." *Jeremiah 30:11.*

It causes us to walk humbly before God as we constantly remember that because of his mercy we are not rewarded according to our iniquities. If we were, we would not be able to stand before him. Sin merits correction, and love sends it, but we are corrected in measure, not according to the desert of sin. Earlier in his prophecy Jeremiah prayed, "O Lord, correct me . . . not in thine anger, lest thou bring me to nothing [diminish me]" (Jer. 10:24). Toward the end of Jeremiah's prophecy the Lord said to him, "I will make a full end of all nations . . . but I will not make a full end of thee, but correct thee in measure; yet will I not leave thee wholly unpunished" (Jer. 46:28).

The discipline of God as the righteous Judge is at once retributive and reformative. David prayed, "O Lord, rebuke me not in thine anger, neither in thy hot displeasure. Have mercy upon me, O Lord!" (Ps. 6:1, 2). So great is God's mercy toward us that he does not deal with us after our sins. With his Father's heart he pities us and corrects us in measure. "Thou our God hast requited us less than our iniquities deserve" (Ezra 9:13). "It is of the Lord's mercies, that we are not consumed, because his compassions fail not" (Lam. 3:22).

As our Father he chastens us, not in full, but in measure; not in wrath, but in love; not to destroy us, but to save us. As his children we are in constant need of his correction, and it would not be right for him never to reprove us. Because God loves us, he rebukes and chastens us. An unidentified author wrote:

> *Father, if Thou must reprove*
> *For all that I have done,*
> *Not in anger, but in love,*
> *Chastise Thy wayward son:*
> *Correct with kind severity,*
> *And bring me home to Thee.*

Like—But Oh How Different!

"Who made thee to differ from another?" 1 Corinthians 4:7.

In an ethnical sense the world's multitudes are alike in that all are descendants of our first parents, Adam and Eve. We are, however, totally different in respect to nationality, color of skin, customs, habits, and religions. Out of over three billion inhabitants of this globe, no two persons can be found exactly alike. One will differ from the other, as one star differs from another in glory. True, in the case of twins of like sex, there may be very strong resemblances; yet a close study will reveal contrasts. John Wesley said that when God fashioned him he broke the mold. Well, there has not been another like this mighty revivalist who became father of the great Methodist Church!

When Paul asked the Corinthians, "Who made thee to differ from another?" he was dealing with gifts and positions in the early church and with those who were somewhat puffed up over their possessions. In respect to the source of the various gifts exercised there was no difference. None could be attained by any personal excellence; all were the free gift of God.

A wide difference is stressed, however, when it comes to one's relationship to God. In this age of grace there is no difference between Jews and Gentiles, for all are sinners and need the same Savior. Upon Israel of old, God laid the necessity of separating the clean from the unclean, putting a difference between them, and likewise between his redeemed people and surrounding nations. The call in this Christian era is to come out from the godless and to be separated unto the Lord. What a vast difference there is between those quickened by the Spirit and made alive unto God and those dead in trespasses and sins! The regret is that the line is not as distinctly drawn as it should be. Little difference is observable between some who confess to be Christ's and those making no profession.

Dear to God, Dearer We Cannot Be

"He that toucheth you, toucheth the apple of his eye."
Zechariah 2:8.

Zechariah, the prophet of hope, loved to dwell upon the infinite tenderness of God in dealing with his people who had been visited with sore judgments, reduced to wretched straits, and left despised. Returning to their own country after a period of captivity in an alien land, the people were like brands plucked from the burning; they were badly scorched. Tears of deep contrition were theirs, and in his love and pity God assured them of future protection and safety. He would guard them as "the apple of his eye."

There is no part of the human frame so safely protected as the apple, or pupil, of the eye. F. B. Meyer, the popular English pastor and speaker who died in 1929, reminded us, "The strong frontal bones, the brow or eyelash to intercept the dust, the lid to protect from scorching glare, the sensitive tear-glands incessantly pouring their crystal tides over its surface—what a wealth of delicate machinery for its safety and health!" We use the phrase "the apple of his eye" to symbolize a most cherished object.

Redeemed by the blood of his Son, the church is God's most cherished object of affection, and he is ever near to defend and cleanse her. Those who persecute the faithful persecute their Master, as Saul of Tarsus, persecuting the church, heard Jesus say, "Saul, Saul, why persecutest thou me?" (Acts 9:4). Seeking to ill-treat the saints, Saul was ill-treating their Savior even though Jesus was in heaven, for his saints and he are one.

Is it not consoling to know that we are as near and dear to Jehovah as the apple of his eye, that safe shelter is ours under the shadow of his wings, as Zechariah further declared? If we are in need of discipline, he will not suffer others to give it to us but tenderly apply it himself. Since we have his kind care, loving sympathy, and constant protection, we should be joyful. How wonderful are the ways of him who has been our help in the past and is our hope for years to come! God's existence is passed in helping weakness.

Such Things As Were Most Precious to Me

"He is precious . . . precious blood." *1 Peter 1:19, 2:7.*

In Shakespeare's *Macbeth* Macduff replies to Malcolm:

> *But I must also feel it as a man.*
> *I cannot but remember such things were*
> *That were most precious to me.*

Laurence Sterne, seventeenth-century essayist, wrote of "Dear sensibility! source inexhausted of all that's precious in our joys, or costly in our sorrows." The adjective *precious* figures often in Peter's vocabulary. He never failed to remember such things as were precious to his heart. The apostle reveled in God's "*precious* promises" (2 Pet. 1:4); in the trial of his faith which was much more *precious* to him than gold, in "the *precious* blood of Christ" (1 Pet. 1:19), in Christ the one "chosen of God, and *precious*" (1 Pet. 2:4), in the possession of a "*precious* faith" (1 Pet. 1:7), and in Christ as being "*precious* to you which believe." To them Christ is "the aroma from life to life" (2 Cor. 2:16). The Revised Version of "He is precious" (1 Pet. 1:7) reads in the Amplified Bible, "For you therefore that believe in the *preciousness.*" He is precious in himself and is the source of all that is precious to the believer. We sing with an unidentified hymn writer:

> *Our Saviour is more precious far*
> *Than life, and all its comforts are;*
> *More precious than our daily food;*
> *More precious than our vital blood.*

As we think of every name he wears, every virtue he bears, every relation he fills, every office he sustains, none can be compared with him. Do you value him above all others, love him as you do no other, prefer him above all things, and consider him altogether lovely and beyond all human wealth and worth? The more you come to know of him, the more you will prize him.

Boundless, Endless, and Sublime

"Is the Spirit of the Lord straightened?" *Micah 2:7.*

In "Childe Harold" Byron eloquently described creation as God's "glorious mirror" in which was seen his form, "boundless, endless, and sublime, the image of Eternity." As the Spirit played a vital part in the creation of our marvelous universe, he can never be straightened in his activities since he too is "boundless, endless, and sublime." His hand is never shortened that it cannot redeem or deliver, nor his ear heavy that it cannot hear the cry of sorrow for sin.

When we think of the vast, unnumbered, unreclaimed multitudes in the world, it would seem as if the power of the Spirit is limited and feeble. If he is omnipotent, then surely the knowledge of God's salvation should have transfigured this sinful world before now. But we are blameworthy, not the Spirit of grace. The church has been straightened, unconcerned, and negligent in her mission to reach earth's millions who cry, "Come and help us, or we die." There are no restraints with God's Spirit when it comes to the evangelization of a lost world. Must we not confess that we have been living far below our privileges as those regenerated and indwelt by the omnipotent Spirit? If his mighty hand is withheld in blessing, the fault is ours, not his.

Have we grieved the Spirit, quenched his operations, sown to the flesh instead of to him, and thereby caused him to restrict his activities? Jesus, the Son of God with power, could not do mighty works because of unbelief; and Israel long ago, by her lack of dedication, "limited the Holy One of Israel" (Ps. 78:41). Without the mighty Spirit we can do nothing, but with him controlling every phase of life there is no limit to what he is able to accomplish through us. This old world has yet to see what he can do through those who give him the unrestricted control of their lives.

Let Me Hide Myself in Thee

"I flee unto thee to hide." *Psalm 143:9.*

Individuals seek refuge from their mistakes, trials, disappointments, and conflicts in different ways. Many drink to hide from their sins and sorrows. Others flee into suicide as the way out of their anguish. Of old, when forced from home through deceit, Jacob fled to Laban; the murderer hastened to a city of refuge provided for the man slayer; Asa sought physicians for relief; Saul, whose refuge was once in God, hurried to the witch; Ephraim in his peril found his way to King Jareb for shelter and help. But the child of God has no other refuge than God himself who is his "refuge and strength" and his "hiding-place." The psalmist, harassed by foes, cried to God, "I flee unto thee to hide me" (143:9).

How Satan outwits himself when he drives us to our God who presents himself as our "shelter in the time of storm"! We are ever in danger from sin, self, and Satan; and fear, painful although groundless, may be ours because we are unable to defend ourselves or to overcome our opposers. Yet what wisdom is ours if we see the storm approaching and make for the covert to hide for safety and comfort. May we be found at all times fleeing to Jehovah who is ever "a very present help in trouble."

Fleeing from the world, the flesh, and the Devil, may we flee to Jesus, for other refuge have we none. His ear is ever open to hear our cry; his heart always yearns to shelter us; his hand is ever ready to deliver and protect . Let us flee to him by prayer in faith and hope for his deliverance. We shall then sing with an unknown hymn writer:

> *Happy soul, that free from harms,*
> *Rests within his Shepherd's arms!*
> *Who his quiet shall molest?*
> *Who shall violate his rest?*

Grow Old Along with Me

"Such an one as Paul the aged." *Philemon 9.*

As I write this meditation, the ninetieth milestone of my life's pilgrimage is not far away. Therefore, I feel qualified to meditate upon old age. Paul was not old in years when he wrote of himself as being "aged," for he finished his course around sixty years of age. But his life of unexampled labor and suffering in prisons and chains, as well as physical disability, made him prematurely old and withered. Thus this reference to being aged has a peculiar beauty and pathos about it and is a stirring appeal to those of us not far from the end of the road.

In his letter to Titus, Paul urged the "older men to be temperate, dignified, sensible, sound in faith, in love, in perseverance" (2:2), and the apostle certainly practiced what he preached. Physical vigor and youth may vanish, but there is a power outside the domain of nature for those who wait upon the Lord for renewal of strength. Caleb, at age eighty-five, drew his spiritual strength from God who was also the source of his courage. Was this not his boast when he said, "As yet I am as strong this day as I was in the day that Moses sent me" [forty years previously] as my strength was then, even so is my strength now" (Josh 14:11)?

If an infirmity has crept over our bodies, we must guard against its creeping over our souls. If our feet cannot take us out into public service as they used to do, there is much work we can do on our knees in spiritual intercession for the church and the world. That most eloquent Scottish divine, James Guthrie, long now with the Lord, once wrote:

> They say I am growing old because my hair is silvered,
> and there are crow's-feet on my forehead, and my step
> is not as firm and elastic as before. But they are mistaken.
> That is not me. The knees are weak, but the knees are
> not me. The brow is wrinkled, but the brow is not me.
> This is the house I live in. But I am young—younger than
> ever I was before.

Are you an aged pilgrim? Then recall Robert Browning's words: "Grow old along with me! The best is yet to be."

The Sweet Omniscience of Love

"Your Father knoweth what things ye have need of, before ye ask him." *Matthew 6:8.*

If this assertion of Jesus is true—and it is—then why waste breath asking God for what he already knows we need? The simple answer is because he said, "Ask, and ye shall receive" (John 16:24). What a precious and consolatory truth there is in this statement found in the Sermon on the Mount!

Your Father. Such a privileged relationship is ours through the finished work of the cross and the regenerating power of the Holy Spirit. Jesus taught his own to look up into the face of God and address him as their Father in heaven. God is not the Father of all. His fatherhood is based upon the Saviorhood of his Son.

Knoweth. Jesus here emphasized the foreknowledge and omniscience of his Father—attributes associated with him throughout Scripture. There is no personal detail—past, present, and future—of your life and mine beyond his ken. Nothing escapes the eye of him whose grace covers our life from commencement to the end.

What things ye need. It will be noted that this means the Father's knowledge of what we need and not our own estimation. All circumstances are minutely and absolutely known to him. Whether the needs are physical, material, or spiritual, he has a register of them all; because of his omnipotence he can meet any need according to his riches in glory. How comforting it is to believe that before the heart can recite its need the loving Father is on his way to meet it!

Before ye ask him. Before we enter his presence with our plea for help, God is cognizant of the burden of our spirit. He has already bottled our tears and recorded beforehand what his omniscient mind knows are our needs. His knowledge is perfect, and our needs are real. When the twain meet, what relief is ours. Let us rest in all he is in himself.

Secret and Insidious Perils

"Moth and rust doth consume." Matthew 6:19.

Jesus was master of the art of simple, easy-to-understand illustrations in his enforcement of truth. He could see "sermons in stones, and books in brooks," as Shakespeare wrote in *As You Like It*. Here, for example, in dealing with the ways treasure can be lost, he suggested that the *moth* and the *rust* represent the more secret, subtle, and insidious perils which eat away slowly and silently at our treasures. What truths do the conjunction of these consumers suggest?

The moth. Looking silky, beautiful, and innocent as it flits about in the twilight of the day, the moth seems a little, harmless, innocent creature; yet what destruction it can cause. It can hide and burrow among costly garments and riddle them with holes until they are only fit to be burned. The moth can stand for what we call little sins, but there is no such thing as a little sin, for sin, no matter how minute we think it is, is sin. Seemingly harmless and innocent thoughts, imaginations, and desires are heedlessly admitted into the inner life and gradually corrupt and consume one's moral and spiritual strength.

The rust. Without doubt, rust is the symbol of neglect. Tools and utensils never rust if kept clean and in constant use. Science has provided us with lotions to prevent rust. The use of talents can be lost through neglect, as Bishop Westcott acknowledged when he said that his absorption in theological studies consumed his gift of song. Negligence is just as destructive as rust and must be guarded against. To neglect God's great salvation is to be in peril of being eternally lost.

Jesus prefaced his warnings against the moth and the rust with the exclamation "Beware!" May he enable us to be ever on our guard against the deadly peril of both. Moth and rust may seem harmless, and therein lies their subtle and most deadly danger. Let us beware of giving shelter to anything, no matter how innocent looking, that would consume us.

The Bounds of Freedom Wider Yet

"The Word of God is not bound." *2 Timothy 2:9.*

Paul found deep satisfaction in calling himself, not a prisoner of any Roman emperor, but "the prisoner of Jesus Christ" (Eph. 3:1) who had permitted his prison chains for the gospel's sake. In the passage before us Paul used his bondage as a striking contrast to the unfettered word he loved and lived to preach. "I suffer hardship unto bonds, as a malefactor; but the word of God is not bound" (2 Tim. 2:9, RV). Roman authority might cast Paul into the dungeon and chain his hands and feet, but it could not prevent the gospel he preached from traveling on its free, untrammeled way. The apostle's foes tried to circumscribe his influence and to retard the spread of the Christian truths he declared, but—and you can feel something of the glow in his heart—he exultantly declared, "The Word of God is not bound!"

Godless persons may imprison those who preach the Word, but they cannot clamp chains upon it or stifle and silence its voice. Because it is God's infallible Word, it must run, have free course, and be abundantly glorified as the Word that liveth and abideth forever.

During the reign of Charles II the state tried to silence John Bunyan by throwing him into Bedford Gaol. But within his cell he wrote *Grace Abounding* and dreamed of *Pilgrim's Progress* which, next to the Bible, enjoys the largest circulation of any Christian book today. From that Gaol the Word for which Bunyan suffered ran on its unfettered way through the world. Communism may silence preachers in cruel ways and try to expel the Word of God from those under the sway of such an atheistic philosophy. But it will yet reveal itself as the unfettered Word, freeing those bound with the chains of their own godless systems of government. Praise God, for his Word that cannot be bound!

God's Nightingales

"In the night his song shall be with me." *Psalm 42:8.*
"God . . . who giveth songs in the night." *Job 35:10.*

The nightingale seems to be one of the favorite birds among poets; many have dwelt upon its characteristic feature of singing in the night. In *Romeo and Juliet* Shakespeare said of this twang-throated singer, "Nightly she sings on yond pomegranate tree." The bard also dwelt on what the nightingale could do if only "she should sing by day." John Higly, of the fifteenth century, wrote, "O 'tis the ravished nightingale . . . Her woes at midnight rise . . . The moon not waking till she sings." Andrew Marvell described the songstress as "sitting so late . . . Studying all the summer night, Her matchless songs doth meditate." John Fletcher, who died in 1625, gave us these lines in his "Faithful Shepherdess":

> *The nightingale among the thick-leaved Spring,*
> *That sits alone in sorrow, and doth sing*
> *Whole nights away in mourning.*

John Milton's frequent references to the nightingale indicate how he loved this bird. He too described its habit of singing in the night in *Paradise Lost:*

> *. . . All but the wakeful nightingale;*
> *She all night her amorous descant sung;*
> *Silence was pleased . . . .*

God too has his nightingales who are able to sing their songs in the night of trial, sorrow, or separation. Paul and Silas, fettered with chains and sitting on the cold floor of their prison cell at the mignight hour, could sing praises unto God whose ear could hear no sublimer music since he gave his human nightingales their songs.

Even when we come to walk through the dark valley of death, the cheerful song of faith is, "Thou art with me." A proverb has it that "a nightingale cannot sing in a cage," but this is not so with those to whom God gives songs in the night. Madame Guyon in prison confinement could pen her wonderful poem:

> *A little bird I am, shut in from fields of air,*
> *And in my cage I sit and sing, to Him who placed me there.*

Have you come to a night of grief and loss? Then let your heart sing unto the Lord.

Perseverance Keeps Honor Bright

"The race is not to the swift, nor the battle to the strong."
Ecclesiastes 9:11.

Among the wise sayings of Solomon none is more eloquent in praise of perseverance than the one before us. Far too many of us start well, but we never get there. We lack what is known as "stickability." Matthew Henry's comment on the passage is significant: "One would think that the lightest of foot should, in running, win the prize; and yet *the race is not* always *to the swift*, some accident happens to retard them, or they are too secure, . . . and let those that are slower get the start of them. One would think that, in fighting, the most numerous and powerful army should be always victorious, and, in single combat, that the bold and mighty champion would win; . . . but *the battle is not* always *to the strong*." Young David in his slaughter of Goliath and the rout of the Philistines proved that the weak can carry the day against formidable power. Frances Ridley Havergal has the line, "The swift is not the safe, and the sweet is not the strong." Prayer and perseverance count in the long run.

The ancient fable by Aesop about the hare and the tortoise illustrates the doggerell we used to sing, "Go on, go on, go on!" The proud hare laughed at the short feet and crawl of the tortoise. But the latter in confidence said, "Though you be swift as the wind I will beat you in a race." The hare accepted the challenge, and they decided that a fox should choose the course and name the goal. Well, the day came for the race, and the hare and tortoise left the starting line together. With its native speed the hare was soon far ahead of the tortoise that lumbered on with a slow but steady pace. Feeling that the race was in the bag, the hare fell fast asleep. Awaking, on he ran, thinking the tortoise was still behind, but on reaching the goal, he found there the tortoise whose perseverance won him the race.

We read that Jesus set his feet steadfastly toward Jerusalem and never halted until he reached there to die upon a tree. Paul could say, "By the grace of God, I am what I am (1 Cor. 15:10). May the same God inspire our perseverance in the race set before us.

36

Bring Me My Chariot of Fire

"There appeared a chariot of fire, and horses of fire."
2 Kings 2:11.

As the result of sin's entrance into the beautiful world God created, countless millions, from Adam and Eve down the ages to the present hour, have passed into eternity through the tunnel of death, with the exception of two godly men, Enoch and Elijah. All persons, whether Christian or unsaved, will continue to leave the world by way of the grave until Jesus returns for his church when all the redeemed, living at that glorious moment, will be caught up to meet the Lord in the air and thus, like Enoch and Elijah, will not taste death.

What are some of the truths to be gleaned from Elijah's sudden, glorious, and dramatic translation to glory? First, he had an inner conviction that he was about to meet the God he had so faithfully served. When persons live in close communion with God, as Elijah did, they become very sensitive to divine purposes. They can catch the whisperings of heaven.

When Elijah's last day on earth came, he spent it quietly doing his work. The companionship of Elijah and Elisha was precious during those last days. Elijah knew that Elisha had a heart like his own and thus wanted him near when his unusual disappearance occurred. When the hour arrived, it seemed to Elisha that twenty thousand chariots surrounded Elijah, along with the angels doing God's bidding as a flame of fire. As the prophet of fire, Elijah had defied Ahab, "The God that answereth by fire, let him be God (1 Kings 18:24). Elijah left earth, not in quiet peacefulness like Enoch before him, but in the whirlwind and the flame of his career into the rest of God.

Elisha not only received Elijah's mantle—the badge of his prophetic calling—but a double portion of his master's loyal spirit. The only eye that saw Elijah in the chariot of fire and caught up to heaven in a whirlwind was Elisha's. The first to see the risen Jesus was Mary. This is the sight love receives. Such love is not blind but has the keenest of all sight.

Sore Let and Hindering in Running the Race

"The spirit suffered them not." Acts 16:7.

The Holy Spirit not only *constrains*, but *restrains*, as Paul proved when he was intent on preaching the gospel, first in Asia and then, when the door was closed, in Bithynia. But as sincere as he was to spread the truth, in both cases, the Spirit of Jesus did not permit Paul to go on his mission. Because of his intimate knowledge of the Spirit's nature and ministry, the apostle doubtless bowed in submission, believing that he knew best.

There are some *hinderings* we can fully understand. For instance, God intervened to prevent Balaam from carrying out his intention to curse Israel. He restrained Herod from fulfilling his cruel purpose to kill the infant Jesus. It seems right for God to bring the devices of the wicked to nought, for such action is in harmony with God's character.

On the other hand, it is hard to understand that some of the disappointments and frustrated good purposes are the work of the Spirit. Paul knew that Asia was a magnificent field for evangelism; yet he was "forbidden of the Holy Spirit to speak the word in Asia" (Acts 16:6). Divine interference thwarted the apostle's plan, but Paul's faith did not break down as, possibly, ours would have done. It is hard for those who are zealous to spread the gospel to understand that the closing of some doors can be the act of a loving God. Because of his omniscience and foresight, he knows best. What we must believe is that God is as truly in the prohibitions, hindrances, and disappointments of life as he is in its fulfillments, joys, and blessings. God is ever thinking upon us for our good, even when he closes a door.

Who Shall Ever Find Joy's Language?

"We joy in God." Romans 5:11.

The whole verse of Robert Bridges in his poem "Growth of Love" is true of divine joy:

> *Ah heavenly joy! But who hath ever heard,*
> *Who hath seen joy, or who shall ever find*
> *Joy's language? There is neither speech nor word;*
> *Nought but itself to teach it to mankind.*

We do not joy in our feelings because they fluctuate and change; we do not joy in our friends, for death robs us of them; we do not joy in our possessions, for they are liable to take wings and fly away. *We joy in God.* Although the exercise of this joy may be more apparent at some times than others, the object of our joy is eternally the same. Thus we joy and rejoice in God as our heavenly Father who cares for us as his children, as our friend who sticks closer than a brother, befriending us at all times, and as the God of all comfort upholding and sustaining us during the trials and sorrows of life.

Such a deep-seated joy, unspeakable and full of glory, is an emotion we cannot produce. It comes to us from God, for "the fruit of the Spirit is . . . joy" (Gal. 5:22). This divine joy is the privilege of every child of God on the basis of the faithful work of his beloved Son at Calvary. All charges against him have been blotted out. He is freely and fully forgiven and justified from all things and stands before God in Christ, accepted, beloved, and blessed. Now, at peace with God and made a son of God, the believer's exceeding joy is God. Can you say that *your* joy is *in* and *from* God? To quote an unknown source:

> *The earthly joys lay palpable, A taint in each, distinct as well;*
> *The heavenly flitted, faint and rare, Above them, but as truly were*
> *Faintless, so is their nature best.*

Well might we pray: Lord, evermore, give us these untainted heavenly joys!

SILENCE
and
REMEMBRANCE

November's sky is chill and drear,
November's leaf is red and sear.

—Sir Walter Scott,
"Marmion"

The Grand Perhaps

"Perhaps he therefore departed for a season."
Philemon 15, 16.

We may not experience that every *perhaps* is "grand," as Robert Browning suggested, but Paul wanted Philemon to know that perhaps Onesimus was parted from him for a while as a servant, that he might have him forever as a brother beloved. Thus for Philemon this would be a "grand perhaps." Now that Onesimus was a Christian, Paul could give some of God's reasons why the one-time slave had forsaken Colosse. But he felt there might be other reasons beyond his knowledge. An unknown poet of the eighteenth century wrote of

> *Dreams that bring us little comfort, heavenly promises that lapse*
> *Into some remote* It may be, *into some forlorn* Perhaps.

But from God's side the mists that seem to hang about many of his intentions and doings are never forlorn. God has his own secret stairs to fulfill his journeys. While uncertainty may be ours, constraining us to say, "Perhaps this is his design" or "It may be this is his purpose," God acts unerringly even though we cannot predict his exact aim. It should be enough that we are in his hands and that with him there are no *perhapses*. He is able to tune the lights and shadows, the joys and griefs, into glorious harmony. We only limit his wisdom and his power if we try to forecast infallibly his methods.

An old Scottish saint cried, "I do not know by what door he will approach. I thought he would come by the way of the hills, and, lo, he came by the way of the valleys!" Dr. Alexander Maclaren's comment on the above verse is worthy of note:

> We are not to be too sure of what God means by such
> and such a thing, as some are wont to be, as if we had been
> sworn of God's privy-council. . . . A humble *perhaps*
> often grows into a *verily, verily*—and a hasty, over-
> confident *verily, verily* often dwindles to a hesitating
> *perhaps.* Let us not be in too great a hurry to make sure
> that we have the key of the cabinet where God keeps His
> purposes, but content ourselves with *perhaps* when we
> are interpreting the often questionable ways of His
> providence, each of which has many meanings and
> many ends.

Trust God: See All, nor Be Afraid

"I will not be afraid of ten thousands of people, that have
set themselves against me round about." *Psalm 3:6.*

The psalmist presented us with many passages urging us to the unreservedness of trust, ever honoring God who loves his people to depend
upon him in simple, childlike confidence. David was not scared by ten
thousands of people although nothing could look worse to human sight
than such an array of enemies. Despite appearances, David had a calm
born of faith. Others might have said, "All these things are against me,
and ruin stares me in the face," but not so the psalmist who, through his
trust in God, had a loophole of escape and could boast, "I will not be
afraid."

Similar circumstances confronted Martin Luther as he journeyed
toward Worms. His dear friend heard that the enemies of the Reforma-
tion were going to treat him as a heretic and sent Luther the message,
"Do not enter Worms!" But he sent back the challenge to his confidant,
Spalatin, "Go tell your master, that even should there be as many devils
in Worms as tiles on housetops, still I would enter it." And as we know,
he did. Luther said, "I was then undaunted, I feared nothing."

How do we act when, in our Christian witness, we find ourselves
surrounded by hostile forces, seen and unseen, as well as adverse
circumstances? If we walk by sight, fear will grip our hearts and defeat
will be ours. If, however, we walk by faith, believing that greater is
he who is in us than the enemy against us, then with all confidence we
can say with David, "I will not be afraid."

To trust only when appearances are favorable is to sail only with
the wind and tide, to believe only when we can see. May ours be that
unreservedness of faith enabling us to trust God come what will. In
triumph Job could confess, "Though he slay me, yet will I trust him!"
(13:15). Let our prayer be, "Lord, give me that unreserved faith enabling me to trust thee unreservedly, despite all appearances. Amen!"

Ingratitude, Thou Marble-hearted Fiend

"Be ye thankful." Colossians 3:15.

That Shakespeare abhorred thanklessness is seen in his frequent condemnation of it. In addition to his description from *King Lear* given in the above title, we have the following song from *As You Like It:*

> *Blow, blow, thou winter wind,*
> *Thou art not so unkind*
> *As man's ingratitude.*

Wordsworth wrote of the lack of gratitude, "It hath oftener left me mourning." Paul said that one evidence of godlessness is, "Neither were thankful" (Rom. 1:21). A trait of godliness is "the giving of thanks."

As those who are the Lord's, we have so much to be grateful for since we are surrounded by mercies—physical, material, temporal, spiritual. As we think of our salvation, are we not thankful that God chose us in his beloved Son before the foundation of the world and that he sent him to be the propitiation for our sins and to make us meet for heaven? How we should strive to live as glad, grateful, and loving children and thereby rejoice the heart of our heavenly Father who emptied heaven of the best for our redemption!

Having his grace in our hearts, his infallible Word in our hands, his mercies in our homes and in our daily lives, we should be found giving thanks continually to his name. May we ever guard against harboring the marble-hearted fiend of ingratitude in our hearts. If thanklessness has been ours, let us confess it before the Lord, mourn over it, and ask him to fill our souls with daily praise for his unmerited grace and goodness. May he enable us to live as thoughtful dependents upon his bounty and as grateful, loving children, praising him from whom all blessings flow. Joseph Addison, the seventeenth-century poet, wrote:

> *Through all eternity to Thee,*
> *A joyful song I'll raise;*
> *For O, eternity's too short*
> *To utter all Thy praise.*

Thy Sweet Converse and Love So Deeply Joined

"I will speak of the glorious honour of thy majesty."
Psalm 145:5.

John Milton was right in joining converse and love, for out of the heart proceeds conversation, whether sweet or sour. Therefore, it is imperative to keep our hearts with all diligence, for out of it are the issues, not only of life, but of lips. Much is said in Scripture about *conversation*. We are to order our conversation aright, to live and labor as becomes the Gospel, to be holy in all manner of conversation, and to be examples of those using chaste conversation.

In some references the word *conversation* implies manner of life rather than, explicitly, the words of our lips. The psalmist had no doubt as to the content of his converse. "I will speak," he said, "of the glorious honour of thy majesty." In general, the habitual converse of the world is low, with buying and selling, gossiping, and trifling matters forming the staple subjects of talk. Those of the earth are earthly, and as their hopes, interests, and enjoyments, so their conversation. Where the treasure is, there will the heart be also; and where the heart is, there generally will be the tongue also. Out of the abundance of the heart, the mouth speaks.

It is not to be supposed for one moment that because we are Christians we must shut out from our conversation all reference to the ordinary affairs of daily life and business, for we have to earn our bread by labor and talk to people of the world. What we have to watch is becoming worldly in our tone or, as Scripture states it, "order our conversation aright" (Ps. 50:23). The psalmist would have us remember that we are not only to speak *to* God but speak *about* him, particularly of "the glorious honour of thy majesty." The word used for *speak* does not mean an occasional reference to all God is in himself, but "speaking at large," not merely "alluding to, incidentally" but "entering into particulars," as though one took delight in expatiating on all that is involved in the majesty and mercy of the Lord. May we never be ashamed to "talk of his doings."

He Has Not Escaped Who Drags His Chain

"Our soul is escaped as a bird out of the snare."
Psalm 124:7.

The escape the Lord makes possible from the snares of the satanic trapper is complete in that the delivered one is also freed from the chains. But those who profess to have escaped condemnation are still in the trap if they drag their chains as the above proverb suggests. The dominant thought of the psalm before us is the perfect help Jehovah provides for his people when they are surrounded by circumstances that would destroy them.

Often through our own disobedience to the revealed Word of God we involve ourselves in entanglements. Unable to extricate ourselves from a perilous position, we are brought to realize that only by divine action can we escape. Whatever temptation may face us, a way of escape is provided. Peter said that only through the knowledge and experience of Jesus as Savior can we "escape the pollution of the world" (2 Pet. 1:4, RV). We are warned to be aware of the wiles of the Devil as he seeks to enslave us. We have no idea how crafty he is and how cleverly he hides his snares. As F. B. Beyer expressed it:

> Quite unexpectedly he begins to weave the meshes of some
> net around the soul, and seems about to hold it his
> captive. And then, all suddenly, the strong and deft hand
> of our Heavenly Friend interposes, as we sometimes
> interpose on behalf of a struggling insect in a spider's
> web. The snare falls into a tangle heap, and the soul
> is free.

I hope that you have the assurance that you have fully escaped from satanic snares and are now as free as a bird in the air. "Make me a captive, Lord, and then I shall be free," wrote George Matheson. To those who prefer captivity in sin and remain blind to their bondage, the solemn question comes, "How shall we escape, if we neglect so great a salvation?" (Heb. 2:3). If they die in their sin, there can be no escape from eternal condemnation.

Faith Shines Equal, Arming Me from Fear

"Believe the Lord your God." *2 Chronicles 20:20.*

Emily Brontë's "Last Lines" prove that she herself was "surely anchor'd on the stedfast rock of immortality." How moving is the first verse in her poem:

> *No coward soul is mine,*
> *No trembles in the World's storm-troubled sphere;*
> *I see Heaven's glories shine,*
> *And faith shines equal, arming me from fear.*

In the believer, faith and fear cannot exist together. Believing that the Lord is almighty, the Christian is armed against fear. David could confess, "God is my refuge and strength, and a very present help in trouble, Therefore will I not fear" (Ps. 46:1, 2). When such "faith shines equal," then we can laugh at impossibilities and cry, "It shall be done." The proper object of our active faith is not God as the God of nature, but God in Christ through whom he is our covenant God, all sufficient, ever propitious, gracious, taking pleasure in us, and ever ready to undertake for us.

Believing in such a God produces peace of heart, zeal, humility, strength to accomplish his will, and deliverance out of every difficulty. So "have faith in God." We first of all receive faith *from* God since it is a gift he bestows upon sinners who accept his salvation. Faith then is an attribute he increases in those who are saved by his grace.

But the aspect of faith our basic text exhorts us to manifest is faith *in* God, an exercise he requires and approves. If Christ returned today, would he find such a faith in our hearts—faith in himself as the sovereign one, faith in his Word as being true and faithful, faith in his presence, knowing that he will never leave us, faith in his power since nothing is too hard for him, faith in his faithfulness which is as steadfast as the mountains and abides forever? "This is the victory that overcometh the world, even our faith" (1 John 5:4) in one who is supreme. Keep believing!

Gladly Would He Learn and Gladly Teach

"Thou art a teacher come from God." John 3:2.

Chaucer's axiom is certainly descriptive of the Lord Jesus who delighted to do the Father's will and who learned many things by obedience to that will. Having come to make the glad tidings of the gospel possible, Jesus manifested great joy of heart as he fulfilled his ministry as a teacher from God. Teaching is ennobled by the fact that all three persons of the Trinity are presented in the character of teachers. Of the Father it is said, "I am thy God that teacheth thee" (Isa. 48:17). "Who teacheth like Him?" (Job 36:22); "He teacheth thee to profit" (Isa. 48:17). Of the Son it is recorded, "He began to do and teach" (Acts 1:1); "He taught men" (Matt. 7:29). Of the Holy Spirit Jesus promised, "He shall teach you all things" (John 14:26); "The Holy Spirit will teach you what to say" (Luke 12:12). Then, after the Ascension of Jesus, the apostles became conspicuous as teachers, found "daily teaching in the temple" (Acts 5:25). Paul gloried in his mission as "a teacher of the Gentiles."

Among the gifts to the church are teachers, with women being exhorted to be "teachers of good things." Nicodemus said that Jesus was a teacher *sent from God*, indicating that Jesus came with all divine authority and divine inspiration. The miracles he performed authenticated that he came to rule by the power of truth, not by the sword. All teachers of the Word, whether in the home or the church, must look upon their mission as being *from* God and essential therefore to be undertaken *for* God.

What glorious victories the patient teaching of Jesus through some three years achieved in the lives of his disciples, as their noble ministry in the Acts proves! At times flesh and blood find the slow, painstaking, persistent teaching hard and disappointing, but in eternity the Great Teacher himself will graciously reward those who were teachers after his example and for him. So whether we have the privilege of teaching in pulpit, Sunday school, or home, may we be found teaching transgressors the ways of the Lord.

Ye Are Living Poems

"We are his workmanship." *Ephesians 2:10.*

In his verses to children Longfellow said:

> *Ye are better than all the ballads,*
> *That ever were sung or said;*
> *For ye are living poems,*
> *And all the rest are dead.*

Living poems! Evidently *poem* was the symbol of saints. In writing to the Ephesians Paul said that they were God's *workmanship*, the Greek word for which is *poema*, transliterated as our word *poem*. If we lack the gift to compose poems, we love to read inspiring, poetical productions. The meter varies in poems in the way that the course of one life differs from another.

The word Paul used for *workmanship* is only used once elsewhere, also by the apostle. It is found in his premise that the universe is a revelation of the power and deity of the Creator, "The things that are made" (Ps. 45:1)—*poema*. The two poetic masterpieces of God are the universe, brought into being by his fiat, "He spake and it was done" (Gen. 1:24), and the born-again believer, "created in Christ Jesus unto good works." In both references *poema* suggests something produced with effort, object, and design.

It is wonderful that all who are in Christ form the highest, finest, and most beautiful expression of his thought and purpose. They are masterpieces upon whom he bestowed his best and therefore surpass his first creation which only cost God his breath. As God's new creation we represent the precious blood of his beloved. As the couplet expresses it:

> *'Twas great to call a world from naught*
> *'Twas greater to redeem.*

We ourselves and our works are of God's poetic creation. Poems as well as poets, we say, are born, not made. A sinner becomes God's poem by the new birth, and thereafter his good works, not of the flesh, but of God, eloquently express the rhythm and music of a divine creation. Are others blessed as they read the verse of your life as God's poem?

No Pains—No Gains

"I know . . . thy labor, and thy patience."
Revelation 2:2.

In his commendation of the church at Ephesus Jesus used two very forceful words for our English word *patience*. He said, "Thou haste borne, and hast *patience*" and "for my name's sake hast *laboured*, and hast not fainted" (Rev. 2:3). *Labor* in the original language implies "suffering" or "weariness," hence, exhausting toil. The word is associated with the term often used to describe the arduous apostolic labors: "Labour in the Lord" (Rom. 16:12); "Labour more abundantly" (1 Cor. 15:10). The thought implied is that there was no easy, leisurely task, but hard labor involving maximum physical strength and energy.

While the word *patience* comes from a root meaning "staying" or "to wait," it does not suggest mere endurance of the inevitable, for Christ could have relieved himself of his sufferings (Heb. 12:2, 3; Matt. 26:53). *Patience* implies the heroic, brave persistence which, as Christians, we are not only to *bear* but to *contend*.

In his sermon "On Patience" Henry Barrow, sixteenth-century English church reformer, defined it as "that virtue which qualifieth us to bear all conditions and all events, by God's disposal incident to us, with such apprehensions and persuasions of mind, such dispositions and affections of heart, such external deportment and practices of life as God requireth and good reason directeth." The words *bear* and *borne* are related to the words Paul used to urge believers to bear each other's burdens. Zeuxis, the fifth-century B.C. Greek artist, was asked why he spent so much labor and patience on a picture. He replied, "I paint for eternity!"

Can we say that we are laborious and patient in light of eternity where rewards are to be given to all who have labored in the Lord and patiently awaited their Master's return? Every person's work is to be tried by fire to test its quality, the standard being "No pains—no gains." Presently we are in constant conflict with evil, but we must never become weary *in* or *of* the contest. Utter devotedness to Christ must be ours, no matter how hard the task or the endurance required.

Habit Rules the Unreflecting Herd

"Accustomed to do evil." *Jeremiah 13:23.*

Jeremiah's indictment of the habitual sinners of his time is a commentary on Wordsworth's axiom about habit ruling the unreflecting herd. One habit followed another until the evil people became fixed or accustomed to their corrupt ways and could no more change their course of life than a leopard could remove his spots. Hannah More of the early nineteenth century gave us this couplet:

> *Small habits, well pursued betimes*
> *May reach the dignity of crimes.*

The following verse is attributed to Charles Reade, a nineteenth-century English writer:

> *Sow an act, and you reap a habit,*
> *Sow a habit, and you reap a character.*
> *Sow a character, and you reap a destiny.*

There are some things we never had to learn and became accustomed to because they were natural. We were made with the ability to breathe, move, cry, eat, and drink. But we were not born with other abilities which have become habits by doing them over and over again.

In many respects we are made up of *habits.* Doing a thing once does not make a habit. "One swallow does not make a summer," but it is on the way to it. May the good Lord deliver us from any bad habit, for only he can break the fetter that binds us. We read that Jesus "went about doing good" (Acts 10:38). He was "accustomed to do good" in contrast to those Jeremiah wrote about as being "accustomed to do evil."

Are we sincere in cultivating good habits that will result in a Christ-like character and a glorious destiny? The ennobling habits of prayer, reading the Bible, and seeking the fellowship of God's people force the world to become strangely dim in the light of his glory and grace. Ours must be a constant watchfulness and a resolute and self-denying effort if we desire to become accustomed to pleasing God.

Tears and Smiles Like Us He Knew

"Jesus wept." John 11:35.

While the Gospels do not mention the smiles of Jesus, they have something to say of his tears. Yet, as C. F. Alexander in his hymn "Once in Royal David's City" goes on to say, "He feeleth for our sadness, He shareth in our gladness." Although there are only three references to his dropping of warm tears, his must have been "a long drip of human tears." When he was only twelve years of age, Jesus declared his God-given mission in the world, only to find that his brothers and sisters did not believe in him. Living in a home in which he was not understood must have cost Jesus many tears. From early manhood, he was a Man of Sorrows.

The shortest and sweetest text in the Bible is "Jesus wept." These two words have been blessed by God to the hearts of countless thousands, for next to the comfort of knowing that he shed his blood for us is reading that he shed tears for his enemies as well as for his friends. When Jesus rode in lowly guise into Jerusalem with Hosannas, "he beheld the city and wept" (Luke 19:41). Those tears of grief and compassion were for a lost city rejecting his love and grace. A few days later, in dark Gethsemane, he shed not only his tears but great drops of blood as "he offered up prayers and supplications with strong crying and tears" (Heb. 5:7). Such a depth of agony we will never understand.

The other occasion of his tears was in Bethany when death claimed his friend whom he loved. Being told that Lazarus was dead, "Jesus wept!" On Olivet he wept for foes resolved and doomed to perish. In the garden his liquid agony revealed what he was enduring for us. At the grave of Lazarus he wept in sympathy with bereaved loved ones. And in all cases his tears were the result of heart anguish for others. No one has ever suffered as much as Jesus did in his own heart. He still offers prayers and supplications since he ever lives to make intercession for us, but without strong crying and tears. For him all tears have been wiped away; yet he is the same sympathizing Jesus and would have us follow his example by weeping for those who weep. Can it be that we have become too dry-eyed?

Fine Nets and Stratagems to Catch Us In

"Surely in vain the net is spread in the sight of any bird."
Proverbs 1:17.

A double meaning is suggested by Solomon's assertion. Some say that no bird is so foolish as to hop into a net which is surely spread for it. While the bird has a little head and little brain, it does not have so little wit as to do that. Others think that Solomon meant to say that even if a bird sees you spread the net it has not wisdom enough to know what it means and will hop into it.

While there may be some doubt as to what Solomon thought the birds might do, there is no uncertainty at all as to the lesson to be gathered from his saying. If we are foolish enough to go into the net of sin, spread by the Devil for our destruction, to gather a few crumbs of worldly pleasure, then we are easily gulled. The word *gull* is said to be derived from birds who come down from the Arctic regions to fish in flocks in our harbors and coasts. They are easily caught. This may be an insult to the gulls who are not so readily gulled as some humans who find their hearts tangled in amorous nets.

Are we not warned of the wiles, or stratagems, of the Devil and told that of ourselves we have no wisdom to detect his shrewdness as the archdeceiver? We are told that he is a "roaring lion" (1 Pet. 5:8). God gave lions their roar so that everybody could keep out of their way. Satan may spread his net in our sight, but he cannot compel us to go unto it. If our ears and eyes are open, he spreads his net in vain. His cleverly laid nets are surrounded with piles of his victims; yet there is deliverance for them as, like fluttering birds, they entangle themselves worse in the meshes. Satan spread nets for Jesus to walk into, but Jesus' anointed eyes could see them. He came to "proclaim deliverance to the captives, and to set at liberty them that are bruised" (Luke 4:18). If we have escaped as a bird out of the snare of the fowler, we should never cease to praise him who rescued us or cease to tell those who are still trapped of the glorious rescue Jesus can accomplish for them.

Hark, the Glad Sound!

"Blessed is the people that know the joyful sound."
Psalm 89:15.

The American Standard Bible gives us this version of our text: "How blessed are the people who know the blast of the trumpet, and shout of joy." This verse is akin to a similar passage: "With trumpets and the sound of the horn / Shout joyfully before the King, the Lord" (Ps. 98:6). The world abounds in sounds. Many are delightful; others are discordant.

Note first the joyful nature of the sound mentioned by the psalmist. How we love the sound of good, inspiring music and of the warbling birds! But there is a sound sweeter than all other sounds reaching the inner ear of the soul. It is the voice singing to us out of Scripture of the love of God in Christ Jesus. As the hymn by Priscilla J. Owens puts it, "We have heard the joyful sound—Jesus saves!" Such a sound is joyful because it tells us how we can be emancipated from sin's guilt and power and made new creatures in Christ.

Second, "Blessed is the people that know." Those who know this joyful sound of sins forgiven are indeed *blessed.* The word *know* implies more than a mere mental comprehension. It includes a deep personal experience. Some people may not hear a joyful sound easily detected by others, either because they are deaf or cup their ears. The godless have ears but hear not simply because they close their ears.

If a treasure were left us in a will, the same would be joyful to hear about, but if we did not claim it or failed to acquaint ourselves with such a fact, then we would lose a blessing. If possessions are willed to us, we must know all about them and believe the provision of the will and stake all that is ours. The same applies to all the precious, spiritual legacies willed to us by the one who died for us. Blessedness and joy become ours as we know of and claim all that is ours through grace.

In Confidence Shall Be Your Strength

"Cast not away therefore your confidence." *Hebrews 10:35.*

Bible references to *confidence* and its cognates are numerous and, taken together, throw much light on the nature and necessity of such a quality. Bishop Charles John Ellicott gave us the reading, "Cast not away therefore your boldness, seeing it hath a great recompence," and then commented, "To *cast away boldness* is the opposite of 'holding fast the boldness of the hope,' Heb. 3:6; the one belongs to the endurance of the faithful servant, the other to the cowardice of the man who draws back, Heb. 3:12, 16, 18. This verse and the next are closely connected: Hold fast your boldness, seeing that to it belongs great reward; hold it fast, for *he that endureth to the end shall be saved.*" Following the usage of the Authorized Version word *confidence,* we have the writer of Hebrews saying, "[We have confidence] to enter into the holy place by the blood of Jesus" (10:19, RV).

In these days of modernistic approach to fundamental truths of Scripture, doubt is cast upon the efficaciousness of the blood of Jesus to remove sin. Its never-failing power to cleanse from all sin is one aspect of confidence we must not throw away. Virgil had a saying, "Nowhere is confidence safe." It is certainly not safe in many theological training centers today. Unfortunately, too many young men learn to doubt the beliefs they once held and enter the ministry believing their doubts. Arthur Hugh Clough gave us this verse:

> *In controversial foul impureness*
> *The Peace that is thy light to thee*
> *Quench not! In faith and inner sureness*
> *Possess thy soul and let it be.*

Our confidence in the articles of the faith, once delivered unto the saints, will often be assailed and sharply tried, but we must seek grace to hold fast to our confidence until the end, knowing that a great reward awaits us for our unshaken trust in all God has revealed in his Word. Without being contentious, we must earnestly contend for the faith, casting none of it away.

Approach My Soul the Mercy Seat

"Rebekah went to enquire of the Lord." *Genesis 25:22.*

After twenty years of marriage Isaac and Rebekah were still childless, but prayer to God prevailed, and the great trial of faith ended. Realizing that there was more than one child struggling in her womb, Rebekah inquired of the Lord. She learned that she would give birth to two children who in turn would become the progenitors of two nations or "two manner of people," namely, the house of Jacob and the house of Esau (Obad. 18).

Rebekah left us an excellent example to imitate. God, of course, commands us to inquire of him. Did he not say, "I will be enquired of" (Ezek. 36:37)? Joshua and his men greatly erred when they failed to ask counsel of the Lord in respect to the deceit of the Gibeonites. When trouble overtook Job and his mind was perplexed over what God had permitted, he approached the mercy seat and prayed, "Show me wherefore thou contendest with me" (Job. 10:2).

Are you disturbed and confused over the trials and disappointments that have come your way? Go and inquire of the Lord. Ask him for the design of your tears, and he will instruct you and unfold the reason *why* the dark threads are as needful as those of gold and silver. A proverb has it, "Too much inquiring is bad." We fail from too little inquiry of the Lord. Although heaven's Inquiry office never closes, we are not persuaded, as we ought to be, that whatever our circumstances or trials may be the ear of the Lord is ever open to hear our request. His hand is ready to undertake for us.

If painful and distressing experiences overtake us, may we not be found despondent or full of complaint over God's providential dealings, but going to a throne of grace, inquiring of the Lord the reason for our chastisement. David is often described as inquiring of the Lord in the varied crises of his life and receiving all necessary guidance and direction. May this be our constant act and attitude.

I Sing the Progress of a Deathless Soul

"The path of the just . . . shineth more and more unto the perfect day." *Proverbs 4:18.*

For the pilgrim with his deathless soul there must be unhindered progress as he journeys from the City of Destruction to the Celestial City. Since he has been justified by grace, his path must be as the shining light that "shineth more and more unto the perfect day." He cannot remain static in his pilgrimage. If he is not going forward, then he is retreating.

Scripture gives us various descriptions of our spiritual progression: It is "of life unto life"; "faith to faith"; "grace to grace"; "from glory to glory"; "face to face"; "from strength to strength"; "from day to day"; and "more and more." Robert Browning could write of "Progress, man's distinctive mark alone." It should be the distinctive mark of the new person in Christ Jesus. Browning also reminded us that:

> . . . *Progress is*
> *The law of life, man is not man as yet.*

We are not what we should be or shall be, but, like Paul, we follow on, for progress is the law of our life in Christ, and his love perfects what it begins. Much is said regarding our growth as the children of God. Our faith should be found growing exceedingly in the grace and knowledge of the Savior and into a holy temple in the Lord. Can we confess that spiritual growth is ours, that our path "shineth more and more unto the perfect day"? The sentiment Isaac Watts expressed should illustrate our progress in eternal matters:

> *Just such is a Christian; his course he begins*
> *Like the sun in the mist when he mourns for his sins,*
> *And melts into tears; then he breaks out and shines,*
> *But when he comes nearer to finish his race,*
> *Like a fine setting sun, he looks richer in grace,*
> *And gives a sure hope, at the end of his days*
> *Of rising in brighter array!*

60

My Great Taskmaster's Eye

"When thou was under the fig tree, I saw thee." *John 1:48.*

It was when John Milton reached the age of twenty-three that he penned the lines:

> *All is, if I have grace to use it so,*
> *As ever in my great Task-Master's eye.*

Joseph Addison gave us this precious verse:

> *The Lord my Pasture shall prepare,*
> *And feed me with a Shepherd's Care;*
> *His Presence shall my wants supply,*
> *And guard me with a watchful Eye.*

Scripture has much to say about the Master's omniscient, ever-open eye. Nathanael, praying under the fig tree, did not know that the watchful eyes of Jesus saw him on his knees and was surprised when Jesus told him, "I saw thee."

We can never hide from the divine eyes as they scan the whole earth. They saw Adam and Eve when they sought to conceal themselves among the trees of Eden; they saw Abraham as he was about to plunge the knife into his son's heart and stopped him; they saw Hagar in the wilderness when she kissed her boy, Ishmael, and left him to die in the agony of thirst, but *her eyes* were opened to see a well of water; they saw Elijah in the lonely cave, and he was startled by the question, "What dost thou here, Elijah?"

Each of us can say of the Lord, "Thine eye seeth *me!*" Omnipresent, he is present everywhere; omniscient, he sees the needs of his redeemed ones no matter where they are. If his eye is on the odd sparrow and marks its fall, then surely, as those he died to save, we are of more value to him than many sparrows. What pains him as his eyes are upon us is that which is contrary to his character and will. Nathanael was praying at his hallowed spot under the fig tree when Jesus beheld him, and his loving eyes beam with delight as he sees you and me in the spot we have hallowed as a little sanctuary. "Thou God seest me!"

You Told a Lie, an Odious Damned Lie

"They kept back part of the price." *Acts 5:2.*

In Shakespeare's *Othello* Emilia uses these condemning lines:

You told a lie, an odious damned lie!
Upon my soul, a lie! a wicked lie!

Byron asked, "What is a lie?" and provided the answer, " 'Tis but the truth in masquerade." The lie Ananias and Sapphira told was most odious and wicked because it was truth in masquerade, for they had professed to have sold all the possessions for the Lord's cause and had given Peter *all* they had received in payment.

The tragic story of these two disciples is that they kept back, for themselves, part of the price received. For lying against the Holy Spirit in this way they were both smitten with sudden death. The doomed deceivers wanted to imitate the complete surrender of Barnabas who sold *all* he had and gave *all* he secured in payment to the Lord. Proudly and plausibly, Ananias and Sapphira presented to Peter a certain part of what their land brought as if it had been the whole amount. But God revealed to Peter their hypocrisy, and a few minutes later they were corpses, lying stiff and cold at the spot where they dropped dead.

The same incomplete obedience and partial dedication was Saul's sin when he declared that he had slain *everything* belonging to Amalek and said to Samuel, "I have performed the commandment of the Lord" (1 Sam. 15:13). But Samuel discerned his lie and said, "What meaneth then this bleating of the sheep in mine ears?" (1 Sam. 15:14). Are we not humbled as we reflect upon such triflings with God? We have professed to have our all on his altar; yet ours was but a partial surrender, only part of the price. May we be saved from acting a lie, and may we ever cherish the tender strings, checking us in the path of falsehood in any vow we may make. May he who is the truth constantly cleanse us from all secret faults.

The Roots of Sin Are There

"Lest any root of bitterness springing up, trouble you."
Hebrews 12:15.

There can be little doubt that the writer to the Hebrews had in mind the solemn warning Moses set before Israel about the sin and terrible punishment of idolatry. He ended with the words, "Lest there should be among you a root that beareth gall and words." These last words are given in the margin as "poisonous herb," implying that the root from which sin springs is not only bitter, but poisonous (Deut. 29:18).

One idol worshiper in a community of believers can bring into it a root of bitter poison. Achan did not suffer alone as a root of avarice; all Israel likewise suffered. Peter also referred to Moses' warning when he exposed Simon Magus, who, above all other men, proved a root of bitter poison in the early church.

A root is hidden in the ground, and we become aware of it only when fruit or flowers appear. When a person with the root of poisonous influence in the heart enters an assembly of believers, its appearance brings disruption and bitterness into the church. An evil root may now lurk hidden in some heart, but when fruit appears, it will bear a terrible harvest of misery to many.

We should be found searching our own souls to discover if there is any root of bitterness growing in the soil. Then, with all prayer and thoroughness, we should root it out before it can spring up to cause trouble to ourselves and to others. A root is always growing as long as it is left living in the ground. By nature it cannot remain inactive but is always spreading out beneath the surface before it reveals itself in branch and leaf. Likewise the longer sin remains in the heart, the stronger it grows and the harder it becomes to kill.

The nature of the fruit corresponds to the nature of the root; if the root is bitter, it produces bitter fruit. But the root can be dealt with drastically and made to bear fruits of righteousness. On the way to Damascus the bitter root in Saul of Tarsus was transformed by a flash of Christ's redeeming love. With the root of a renewed nature implanted, Saul became the greatest figure in the New Testament next to Jesus who himself was a root out of the dry ground.

The Last Enemy Destroyed by Emmanuel

"O grave, I will be thy destruction." *Hosea 13:14.*

Among ancient Greek stories is this one about the city of Athens doomed to supply each year a tribute of youths and maidens to the monster of Crete. However, the hero Theseus embarked with the crew and accompanied the victims that he might beard the dreadful ogre in his den and, slaying him, forever free his native city from the burden of death under which it had groaned.

Did not the prophet Hosea predict the victory of Jesus, our heavenly Theseus, when he affirmed that he would deliver from the power of the grave? "O death, I will be thy plague! O grave, I will be thy destruction" (13:14). Is this not the same paean of victory Paul joined in when he exclaimed, "O death, where is thy sting? O grave, where is thy victory?" (I Cor. 15:55).

When Jesus clothed himself with the garment of our humanity it was with the glorious purpose of becoming *Death's* death, and, at Calvary, by dying, death he slew. Now the saint can sing, "The fear of death has gone forever." In the Revelation of Jesus Christ afforded the Apostle John, Jesus is depicted as having the keys of death hanging at his girdle, indicating that all power is his to shut so that none can open, and to open so that none can shut. How blessed it is to know that the hour is not far distant when death, as the last enemy, is forever vanquished by him, who was dead, but is now alive forevermore! Till then, when we come to walk through the valley of the shadow of death, we have no fear, for the Deathless One himself is with us to lead us to his heavenly abode in which there is no death. Evan Hopkins wrote:

> *Work on, then, Lord, till on my soul*
> *Eternal Light shall break,*
> *And, in Thy likeness perfected,*
> *I "satisfied" shall wake.*

A Wise and Masterly Inactivity

"Their strength is to sit still." Isaiah 30:7.

This title is taken from a speech by Sir James Mackintosh, Scottish philosopher and historian who died in 1832, in which he said, "The House of Commons, faithful in their system, remained in a wise and masterly inactivity." Isaiah would have us experience the strength gained from a certain form of inactivity, namely, sitting still—a great trial for those who are mad in their pursuit for action or who must always be "up and doing." Theirs would be great achievement if only they could learn to be "down and dying to self-energy."

Isaiah recorded how the Jews wanted to have a sense of security in the midst of their foes and sought to get it by forming an alliance with their ancient masters and oppressors on the bank of the Nile. Displeased at this effort, God told his people that the strength of Pharaoh would be their shame, and their trust in the shadow of Egypt, their confusion. Such a security as they sought would not profit them. Their strength could only be found by sitting still under God's protection and providence.

To *sit still* does not imply an idle bodily composure but a humble dependence upon God, in contrast to wandering about seeking help from various sources. Those who put their confidence in any creature rather than in the Creator will sooner or later find it a reproach to them. Martha was "careful and cumbered" (Luke 10:40) about many things, but her sister Mary found her strength sitting at the feet of Jesus. Moses assured Israel of divine deliverance when escape from the Egyptians seemed hopeless. "Fear ye not, stand still, and see the salvation of the Lord, which he will shew you today" (Exod. 14:13). All the people could do was to "stand still," facing, as they were, graves in the sea. Standing still did not mean physical inactivity, for God commanded the people to "go forward," but he implied trust in the divine promise, "The Lord shall fight *for* you, and ye shall hold your peace" (Exod. 14:13). Spiritual strength is ours as we wait *before* the Lord and wait *for* him to work.

Be Famous Then by Wisdom

"Four things which . . . exceeding wise." *Proverbs 30:24.*

The wise and their wisdom form favorite themes for poets. For instance, John Milton had much to say about them. Here is a greatly admired verse of his:

> *The childhood shows the man,*
> *As morning shows the day. Be famous then*
> *By wisdom, as thy empire must extend,*
> *So let extend thy mind o'er all the world.*

Solomon, remarkably endowed by God with wisdom, included the saying of another wise man, Agur, in his Proverbs. Ants, conies, locusts, and spiders were cited by Agur as being "little upon the earth, but they are exceeding wise."

Ants have the instinct to prepare for winter, and thus they gather their food in summer for future needs. Unfortunately, many humans are not so wise as the small ants. Time, money, and strength are wasted, and when the winter of trial or of old age comes, help has to be sought from others. Have you been wise enough to prepare for eternity?

Cronies may be a "feeble folk, yet make they their houses in the rocks." These wise creatures, similar in their habits to wild rabbits, make their homes in stony places where their enemies cannot reach them. Instinct and experience prompt other creatures as well to seek the safety of strong places. Has wisdom been ours to find in God our refuge and hiding place? In the East locusts are large and travel in companies. If they were few in number, they would have little power; so they are wise enough to stay and work together. In their unity there is strength.

We usually shun spiders, but the fourteenth-century liberator and king of Scotland, Robert Bruce, in his cave learned the lesson of perseverance by watching a spider try again and again to weave its web. When things are difficult think of the wise spider.

If we would be as wise as serpents, our highest wisdom can only be found in "the only wise Saviour" (Jude 25), who has been made to us "the Wisdom of God" (1 Cor. 1:24).

Such Are the Gates of Paradise

"Go through, go through the gates." *Isaiah 62:10.*

From the first reference to gates in Scripture—Lot sitting in the gate of Sodom (Gen. 19:1)—to the last reference of the twelve gates of pearl which John described in the Book of Revelation, gates of all sorts are mentioned hundreds of times. In our meditation let us think of some gates we ourselves must go through. First, there are gates which God arranges for us to go through whether we will or not, namely, the gates of life and death. At birth we enter the gate of life, and the one who tenderly brought us through this one will graciously lead us through the gate of death to himself if we have entered the new life in Christ.

Next there are gates we must shun, namely, the world, the flesh, and the Devil. To go willingly through these three gates ultimately means going through the gates of hell. John Bunyan in his dream saw that there was a way to hell, even from the gates of heaven.

Third, there are gates we should strive to enter. Jesus used the illustration of two gates open to all sinners, the narrow gate leading to eternal life and the wide gate through which the unrepentant go to eternal condemnation. Faith is one of the principal gates into peace with God, as is prayer. Tennyson wrote of "battering the gates of Heaven with storms of prayer."

Then mention must be made of two gates that shut us in for eternity, that close forever behind us. In his portrayal of the rich man and Lazarus in eternity Jesus emphasized how the gate was barred for each in their respective spheres. "There is a great gulf fixed: so that they which would pass from hence to you cannot; neither can they pass to us, that would come from thence" (Luke 16:26). The pearly gates of paradise exclude "dogs, and sorcerers, and idolators" (Rev. 22:15) forever from eternal bliss and encircle forever all those who obey the call, "Go through, go through the gates" (Isa. 62:10) into the joy of the Lord. How blessed we are if we have entered the open gates of his righteousness!

He Did Entreat Me Past All Saying Nay

"But they constrained him, saying, Abide with us."
Luke 24:29.

This precious portion of Scripture records one of the distinct appearances of Jesus after his resurrection and is one of the most moving passages in the four Gospels. Two disciples had been at Calvary and witnessed the bitter end. Full of sorrow, they journeyed home to Emmaus, some seven miles from Jerusalem where Jesus died. They were companions in grief and were doubtless rehearsing all they could remember of Jesus' life, teaching, suffering, and death.

While thus communing, the two sad men were joined by a stranger, but they did not recognize him as the one they were mourning, for "he appeared in another form." Asking them about the subject of their conversation, Jesus, although he knew what it was all the time, heard from their lips the story of his last hours and of how crushed their hopes were by his death. Then came our Lord's matchless exposition concerning himself, and the two men were at their village before they knew it. Jesus "made as though he would have gone further." This pretense on his part does not imply anything false. He *was* going on and would have gone on but for the entreaty to tarry with them. "They constrained him, saying, Abide with us." They pressed him not to go on his journey. The Lord loves to be entreated by his people.

Ruth said, "Intreat me not to leave thee." Gideon said to the illustrious angel, "Depart not hence, I pray thee." This repeated plea, "I pray thee," proves that the Lord, in love, often tries our faith as he appears to go on. When the invitation came "Abide with us," Jesus responded, and a glorious revelation came to those willing to give him shelter. Those two disciples could not bring themselves to part with one who had done so much for them.

While "Abide with Me" has become the most popular of our evening hymns, we do not have to entreat Jesus to remain, for we have his own promise, "I will never leave thee, nor forsake thee." Read backwards, it means the same, "Thee forsake, nor thee leave, never will I."

Human Nature's Daily Food

"Give ye them to eat." Matthew 14:16.

In the Anglican church there is a Sunday observed in the middle of Lent, forty days before Easter, which is known as Refreshment Sunday. It is so called because in the Gospel reading for the day there is something about people resting in the fields, eating divinely provided food they found refreshing and nourishing. It is the miracle of Christ feeding the five thousand.

Miracles are shadows telling us of something spiritual behind them, and the miracle Jesus performed at the close of a busy day was a parable of all he is as the bread of life. There was *the recognition of need*, for the Master said, "They have nothing to eat" (Mark 8:2). He knew the multitude who had followed him would starve if food were not forthcoming. He is still concerned about the natural daily food of his own and taught us to pray, "Give us this day our daily bread."

Then there was *the recognition of order* in performing the miracle, for Jesus commanded the people to "sit down in groups in order" (Luke 9:14). If the thousands present had been allowed to be all jumbled up together, serving them would have been a hard task. That day Jesus revealed that order is heaven's first law. Are we not enjoined to walk orderly?

Further, there is *the recognition of the use of what we have*. The villages were too far away to buy food, and the disciples produced the five loaves and two fishes found among them. With these a miracle was performed that satisfied the hunger of a vast crowd. Little is much if God is in it, and that day God the Son multiplied what a boy gave him. If we have one talent and fully devote it to him, he will increase it to ten talents. Why not let him make much of the little we have?

There was also *the recognition of waste*, for the fragments of food were gathered into twelve baskets for use later on. Jesus was careful about those "leftovers." Should we not shun any willful waste? The axiom has it, "Waste not, want not!"

Last, there is *the recognition of himself* as the one who is able to feed our souls as we feed our stomachs. Does he not feed us with himself and with his promises? Well might we pray, "Lord feed me, or I'll die."

71

Shining Ones, Whose Faces Shone As the Light

"Shine as lights in the world, holding forth the word of life." Philippians 2:15, 16.

Doubtless all of us are familiar with the description John Bunyan gave in *Pilgrim's Progress* of Christian and Hopeful drawing near to the deep river of death where they met two shining ones whose raiment shone like gold and whose faces shone as the light. Being thus illuminated, they were able to lead the two pilgrims into the city as they emerged from the river. Bunyan was not portraying angels in his figure of "shining ones," but all saints who should shine as lights in the world. The sphere in which they are to shine is a whole world lost in the darkness of sin.

As Jesus was about to leave his disciples, he prayed, not that they should be taken out of the world, but left in it to witness, whether in darkest heathenism or in the dark places of the city where we live. Absence of light not only means darkness but *danger*, as we experience when a blackout occurs because of electrical failure. The question is, Are we—you and I—helping to banish the spiritual darkness in the little piece of the world we represent?

Then it is also necessary to think, not merely of the place where the light is to shine, but of *what* the light is in itself. The word Paul used for *lights* means "luminaries" and it is the same word found at creation, "Let there be lights in the firmament of heaven" (Gen. 1:14). We are to shine as the stars that come twinkling one by one from out the azure sky, scattering beams of grace to all around us. The sacred light we shine with is not self-created but comes from him who declared himself to be "The light of the world" (John 8:12). Our light then is reflected and "shining more and more unto the perfect day." Paul makes it clear that the manner of our shining is associated with the Word of life. We are to *hold forth* as a lamp to our feet and a light to our path.

God made the sun, moon, and stars to shine for the benefit of his world, and as his new creation, we are to display the illuminating Word so that it can be seen by those who are perishing in the darkness of sin and who are in danger of eternal darkness. Have you been a star in someone's sky?

Do It and Make Excuses

"They all with one consent began to make excuse."
Luke 14:18.

The ancient proverb, used as the title for this meditation, is so true of those cited in the Bible as having made excuses, for they indulged in an act of disobedience and then, when exposed, excused themselves. The first one in the world to make an excuse was the first man, Adam. Forbidden by God to touch the tree of knowledge, Adam and Eve tasted of its fruit. Then, smitten with conviction, they foolishly tried to hide from God. Called from his hiding place, Adam crept out and heard the question, "Hast thou eaten of the tree?" (Gen. 3:11). His excuse was ready: Eve gave me the fruit; it is not my fault. Then God looked at Eve. She too had thought up her excuse and said, "The serpent, the wicked serpent beguiled me and I did eat" (Gen. 3:13). From then on we have a succession of "their thoughts the mean while accusing or else excusing one another" (Rom. 2:15), as Paul put it.

No matter how good an excuse, it is impossible to persuade oneself, and very rarely anyone else, that the excuse is truth. An anonymous poet has left us these lines:

> *Oftentimes the excusing of a fault*
> *Doth make the fault worse by the excuse;*
> *As patches set upon a little breach*
> *Discredit more a hiding of the fault*
> *Than did the fault before it was so patched.*

The Duke of Wellington is credited with having said that a person good at making excuses is seldom good for anything else. This is certainly true of those Jesus described as being invited to a great supper but who with "one consent," or all alike, came up with excuses which were disguised lies. As those who profess to be the Lord's, *excuses* is a word that should not be in our vocabulary. If we have erred, it is folly to excuse ourselves. It is better to confess our fault and claim anew the blood of Jesus who is able to cleanse us from all sin.

Be Swift in All Obedience

"According to all that God commanded Noah, so did he."
Genesis 6:22.

Noah will ever remain, not only as a model worker, but as a sterling example of obedience to God, for in accordance to the divine command, this man who walked with God crossed every *t* and dotted every *i*. Although he was not a shipbuilder, living in a seaport town Noah was commissioned to build a large ship the like of which had never been heard of before. How easy it would have been for Noah to make excuses and to reply truthfully to God, "I know nothing about building ships, nor do my sons, and there are no ship carpenters around I can engage to help me." But Noah did not raise the slightest objection and went to work at once. Implicitly, he obeyed God and fashioned the ship, or ark, to divine specifications.

To the godless around, the story of a coming flood and the ship in building to be the means of escape for Noah and his family seemed an idle tale. They must have thought godly Noah a bit of a nut, but on he went in a fearless way to obey God. We read four times that "as God commanded Noah, so did he." Willing to obey God, he found that nothing was too hard for him, and as with Paul, Noah proved that he could do all things through him who strengthened him for his gigantic task.

Have we learned that God's commands are his enablings, that what he asks of us he always imparts strength to obey? "Faithful is He Who called you, *Who also will do it*" (1 Thess. 5:24). One day Charles Wesley said to his famous brother, "If I had a pair of wings I would fly away." John Wesley replied, "If God told thee to fly, he would give thee a pair of wings."

May we never be found saying *I can't* to anything God tells us to do. At the marriage in Cana, Mary, the mother of our Lord, said to the servants of the house, "Whatsoever he saith unto you *do it*" (John 2:5). And they did, helping thereby in the miracle of turning water into wine. With Shakespeare in *Henry VIII* may we learn to say:

> *The will of heaven be done, and the King's pleasure*
> *By me obeyed.*

Little Things Are Infinitely the Most Important

"By little and little." *Exodus 23:30.*

Both Scripture and human experience agree with Arthur Conan Doyle who wrote, "It has long been an axiom of mine that the little things are infinitely the most important." By little and little the Canaanites were driven out of their land by the Israelites; and your heart and life and mine are what Canaan was when the Israelites succeeded—full of wild beasts, or lusts, evil thoughts, and desires. But little by little as God's sanctifying grace works in us, more of the territory of our lives becomes his. We must guard against those little sins and faults that spoil Christian character—the little foxes that spoil the grapes. We must not look with suspicion and even contempt upon that which is outwardly insignificant. It is folly to despise the day of some things.

The whole record of great scientific discoveries and inventions suffices to show that the apparently trivial may be of vast importance. The falling of an apple led to the discovery of the law of gravitation; the steam issuing from a kettle was the starting point of the steam engine. Greatness of little things can also be seen in nature as Julia Fletcher Carney wrote:

> *Little drops of water, little grains of sand*
> *Make the mighty ocean, and the pleasant land.*

Tennyson wrote of how he came "to be grateful at last for a little thing." Are we? Bethlehem-Ephratah was little among the thousands of Judah; yet out of it came the mighty ruler. That little things count in human life was suggested by Hannah More in these lines:

> *The sober comfort, all the peace which springs*
> *From the large aggregate of little things;*
> *On these small cares of daughter, wife, and friend,*
> *The almost sacred joys of home depend.*

Wordsworth would have us remember:

> *That best portions of a man's life*
> *His little, nameless, unremembered acts,*
> *Of kindness and of love.*

76

A Portion of the Eternal

"The Lord is my portion." Psalm 119:57.

One of the most wonderful aspects of our Lord's being is that each of us can look up and claim him as our own. The humblest believer can turn his eyes upon him and say, "Thou art *my* portion, O Lord." The king of Babylon graciously provided for Jehoiachin "every day a portion . . . all the days of his life" (Jer. 52:34). Is Jesus your daily portion, the one you appropriate for the needs of each day? Too many try to exist on a very meager portion of him who is ever ready to bless us with his fullness. Describing the position of the enduring dead when they awake, Shelley affirmed that they will become "a portion of the Eternal." But are not these redeemed by the blood, whether on earth or in heaven, a portion of the eternal? "The Lord's portion is his people," declared Moses (Deut. 32:9). As we by faith endeavor to possess all we have in him, in like manner he is never satisfied until he possesses all we are and have. Are we giving him a full portion to feed upon? It is consoling to sing the words written by Anna L. Waring:

> *"Thou art my Portion," saith my soul,*
> *Ten thousand voices say,*
> *And the music of their glad Amen*
> *Will never die away.*

But can he turn to you and me and say with sublime music in his voice, "Thou art *my* portion"?

DEATH
YET LIFE

In a drear-nighted December,
Too happy, happy tree,
Thy branches ne'er remember
Their green felicity.

—John Keats, *Stanzas*

My Mind Aspire to Higher Things

"Friend, go up higher." Luke 14:10.

Tennyson agreed with Sir Philip Sidney's aspiration for "higher things," for in his *In Memoriam* we have these impressive lines:

> *I held it truth, with him who sings*
> *To one clear harp in divers tones,*
> *That men may rise on stepping-stones*
> *Of their dead selves to higher things.*

Spiritual elevation should be our constant aim as expressed in the well-known hymn by Sarah F. Adams, "Nearer, my God, to Thee, Nearer to Thee."

We fail to bear in mind, however, that humiliation is the ladder to elevation, that to go up higher we must be willing to go down lower. Jesus took upon himself the form of a servant and humbled himself to the brutal death of a cross, but thereafter he was highly exalted and given a name above every name. If we are to go up higher, we must die to self-praise and self-dependence and become more distressed over our spiritual penury.

Ours must be a separation from the world in so far as its godless pleasures and practices are concerned. We cannot climb higher if the things of earth are not growing dim in the light of his glory and grace. Contamination prevents elevation. Matthew Henry's comment is apt: "The way to *rise high*, is, to *begin low*. Thou shalt have honour and respect before those that sit with thee. . . . Honour appears the brighter for shining *out of obscurity*."

A parable from an ancient source says that three men were bidden to a feast. One sat highest, "for," said he, "I am a prince." The other, next, "for," said he, "I am a wise man." The other, lowest, "for," said he, "I am a humble man." The king, seated at the head of the table, placed the humble man highest and put the prince lowest. As God ever delights in exalting those of low degree, may he always find us low at his feet, recognizing that without him we are nothing, have nothing, and can do nothing. Only thus can we rise higher.

Treasure of Light in Earthen Vessels

"Empty pitchers, and lamps within the pitchers."
Judges 7:16.

What a stirring chapter this is in the Book of Judges! In Israel's sad days God raised up Gideon, and thousands flocked to follow his brave leadership. Out of the thirty thousand soldiers he chose three hundred, and dividing them into three companies, he gave each man a ram's horn and an earthen pitcher or vessel with a light hidden in it. At midnight Gideon grouped his valiant three hundred around the tents of Midian and Amalek and silently and unseen moved them closer and closer to the sleeping foes. Then, when Gideon blew a great blast on his own horn, every man did the same, and all cried, "The sword of the Lord and of Gideon" (Judges 7:18). All broke their pitchers, and the lights flashed forth. The robber army was startled from sleep by the sound of the horns and shouting, and seeing the flashing lights moving through the darkness, they were overtaken by panic and fled, only to be pursued by Gideon's band and killed. This is the great victory the gallant judge achieved for Israel.

One wonders whether Paul had this incident in mind and applied it when he wrote: "God, who commanded the light to shine out of darkness, hath shined in our hearts, to give the light of the knowledge of the glory of God in the face of Jesus Christ. But we have this treasure [treasure of light] in earthen vessels, that the excellency of the power may be of God, and not of us" (2 Cor. 4:6, 7). The pitcher, the outflashing of the lights at night, and the excellent power that gained the victory hold a precious lesson for our hearts. Poor, weak, and fragile though we may be, as vessels we carry a divine light and life which cannot be destroyed and which can shine worth and win glorious victories for God who is able to fill the weakest with strength for his work. In ourselves we are vessels of neither gold nor silver, but of clay, like earthen vessels. Yet, when the excellent light and power of God are revealed through us, what marvelous things are accomplished.

Prayer is the Breath of the Soul

"Pray without ceasing." I Thess. 5:17.

Christians cannot live, naturally, without constantly breathing. So, too, they cannot live, spiritually, without prayer, which is their vital breath and native air. And they should be encouraged as they remember that God's ears are ever open to listen to their unceasing petitions. What Paul was doubtless teaching the Thessalonians was the necessity of cultivating the habit of prayer, that as their needs were constantly returning, so their intercessions should be constantly ascending to him who is always ready to listen and answer according to his own wisdom and word.

Does not our prayer-hearing and prayer-answering Father in heaven beseech us to look to him for all our needs and assure us that if what we ask for is according to his will, then it is as pleasant for him to answer our prayers as it is to listen to them? Does he not invite, exhort, and command us to pray always and in everything? But we are so slow to learn that every object that meets the life, every circumstance that occurs, every act in which we engage can afford matter for prayer, if properly viewed. If prayer is allowed to dwindle into a mere duty or into cold, stereotyped forms, occasionally offered, or if it becomes more of a burden than a blessing, then we are heading for spiritual death. Because prayer is the breath of the soul may it become easy for us to pray and as naturally and as constantly as it is to breathe God's fresh air all around us. If we would be spiritually healthy, we must never relax our breathing exercises, particularly in the morning ere we face the heat and burden of the day.

The Irish hymn writer, James Montgomery, sang:

> *Prayer is the Christian's vital breath,*
> *The Christian's native air,*
> *His watchword at the gates of death;*
> *He enters heaven with prayer.*

You May Be Mistaken

"The Lord is God of the hills, but he is not the God of the valleys." *1 Kings 20:28.*

Oliver Cromwell, in a letter to the General Assembly of the Church of Scotland in 1650, wrote, "I beseech you, in the bowels of Christ, think it possible you may be mistaken." The best of persons make mistakes. In his speech at the Mansion House, London, 1899, Edward John Phelps said, "The man who makes no mistakes does not usually make anything." The only person the world has ever known who never made a mistake was the Lord Jesus.

King Ben-hadad, ruler of the Syrians, made a colossal mistake as he discovered to his cost when he declared that the God of the hills was not the God of the Valleys. The king went against a small handful of God's people, and they defeated him, causing him to flee. Ignorantly, Ben-hadad put his reverse in battle down to the fact that it had been fought on the hills. Returning with a larger army and keeping away from the hills, he kept to the valleys, doubtless with the idea that he would be keeping out of the way of Israel's God. But again he was routed and made to escape for his life. Thus two defeats forced Ben-hadad to believe that God is not only the God of the hills, but of the valleys also.

The king's mistake of thinking God is in one place and not in another is a common one today. There are those who think God is in the church but not in their business, and they often act as if God were not omnipresent and omniscient. There is no place where God is not, whether it be hills or valleys. David asked, "Whither shall I flee from thy presence?" (Ps. 139:7), and answered his own question by saying that if he took the wings of the morning to fly to uttermost parts he would find God waiting for him there. In the desert with only a stone as a pillow, fleeing Jacob had a dream that God was in *all* places. When he awoke, he confessed, "Surely the Lord is in *this* place; and I knew it not" (Gen. 28:16). My friend, whether you be on the mountaintop sparkling with light or in the valley of shadows, remember that God is round about you.

All Chance-Direction Which Thou Canst Not See

"And a certain man drew a bow at a venture."
1 Kings 22:34.

What we call *chance* means the way things fall out, leaving things to risk, probability. But Alexander Pope reminded us that a chance can be a direction we cannot see. John Milton would have us think of:

That power
Which erring men call Chance.

What the captains, with their special commission to kill the king of Israel, failed to do, a Syrian common soldier accomplished. Taking aim at one of the enemy, the soldier drew a bow by chance, and away the arrow sped, piercing not another ordinary soldier but the king of Israel himself.

Often our words and deeds are like that Syrian soldier, shooting chance arrows, well-aimed at something but striking a target we had not expected—God giving them a direction we could not see. Doubtless, if the soldier who drew a bow at venture had been told that he would shoot the king and win the battle, he would have laughed and said, "Not I!"

Is this principle not often seen in the things we do? Some of the greatest consequences come out of the smallest chance actions. Invading Scotland, the Danes prepared for a night attack on the sleeping garrison, and all of them crept forward barefooted, but one of the Danes stepped on a large thistle which made him cry out. That cry aroused the sleeping Scottish soldiers, and springing to arms, they drove the Danes back. What we must learn from that Syrian soldier is that there are really no unimportant deeds or words. An unkind word may escape our lips without any purpose on our part really to hurt anybody, but it goes like a poisoned arrow into another heart. The arrow hits a mark we did not expect. Of this we can be certain: if all the arrows we shoot are kind, helping, Christlike words and actions, direction from heaven will guide them to beneficial ends.

Dig for Victory

"Make this valley full of ditches." 2 Kings 3:16, 17.

During World War II enemy action destroyed many ships bringing food to Britain from various parts of the world. People were forced to use food ration books, and a popular national slogan was "Dig for Victory." Gardens, fields, and almost every green patch were made to produce the necessary vegetables for consumption. It was something like this in Elisha's time when a large army, shut up in a dry and thirsty valley, was commanded by God to dig ditches to hold water. The people had to dig in faith, for there was no trace or sign of rain or water anywhere to fill the trenches once dug. But the prophet said dig, assuring them that God would fill the valley ditches, which he did for "the country was filled with water."

Have we discovered that our main business in life is to dig ditches in dry valleys? It is useless to sing "Showers of blessings we need" if trenches in life have not been cut to receive the heavenly supply. In the Lord's parable, the unjust steward who had wasted his goods and faced famine said, "I cannot dig" (Luke 16:3). But he got down to his spade and dug himself out of difficulties.

Are we digging trenches in our own hearts and in the lives of the children at home and in Sunday school that can be filled with the water of life, strengthening ourselves and preparing others to breathe the air and share the blessedness of heaven? Surely no task is comparable to that of preparing channels through which the Spirit of God may flow into our own hearts and through them to others. There may be no cloud in the sky, no sound of wind, no evidence of water anywhere, but as we *dig* in faith, making every preparation for revival, the *deluge* will come. God has promised to fill our trenches with that water which if any man drink he will never thirst again. What a solemn responsibility it is to prepare the way of the Lord.

An Ancient Timekeeper

"The dial of Ahaz." 2 Kings 20:11.

The clever Chaldeans are credited with being the first to invent the sundial to help them by day; at night they reckoned time by observing the movements of the stars. Now we have all kinds of timekeepers which are a vast improvement on the sundial which had to be fixed properly, with its finger pointing toward the north, if correct time were needed. Many of these old sundials can still be seen in churchyards, in old church towers, and in ancient marketplaces. Usually, these dials carry mottoes from which we can gather spiritual lessons. Many of these mottoes indicate the limited use of dials: "I do not take account of the hours unless they are bright"; "I reckon only the sunny hours"; "What's the good of a sundial in the shade?" Since dials require plenty of sun, they are of no use on dull days, and, of course, they are useless at night. Certainly, it is good to look on the bright side of life, but human experience is made up of both sunny hours and dark and gloomy ones.

Another quotation on many a dial is *tempus fugit*, meaning "time flies." The shadow moving along the dial reminded everybody that time did pass away, and that it was incumbent upon them to be on time and to make the most of time, or, as the Bible puts it, "Redeeming the time" (Eph. 5:16).

For King Hezekiah the finger on the dial of Ahaz went back ten degrees as a sign that he would not die but would live another fifteen years. As a guide in life, the dial is disappointing because of its variableness. It may teach us to live admirably in the sunshine but does nothing to prepare us when trouble comes. It may tell accurately the time of day when the sun shines, but its company is no good when night falls. As creatures of time we need a guide without limitation who is able to direct us in the darkest hour as well as in the brightest. We have such a guide in him who has promised to guide us with his eye. Another dial has a Bible text as its motto which we must make our own. "Yet a little while is the light with you. Walk while ye have the light" (John 12:35).

A Little Boy Who Was King

"Josiah was eight years old when he began to reign."
2 Kings 22:1.

Josiah was only a child of eight when he became the king to rule over the Jews. This youngest king in Israel's history has a parallel in English history in Edward VI who was sometimes called the "Josiah of England" since he became king at nine years of age. Like Josiah, Edward had a reverence for God and his Word. As a boy he saw somebody get a large Bible to stand on, not being tall enough to reach something on a shelf, and the young king said, "You must not stand upon the Bible, it is God's Book." What a joy it would be if only we could see more boys—and men—loving and honoring the Bible and treating it with the reverence it deserves.

Both Josiah and Edward VI, who became kings in early life, turned out to be the best of kings. Josiah had a wicked father, Amon, but a very good mother, Jedidolah, who doubtless had a good share in her noble child's doing that which was right in the sight of the Lord. For those who are surrounded by the young, whether at home or in Sunday school, it is imperative to remember that young children can be brought to reign in life by Jesus Christ.

Josiah was eight years old when he began to reign, and in the eighth year of his reign he *began* to seek after God, that is, when he was fifteen years of age. From childhood Josiah had loved everything about God. Loving God's house, then in a bad state, he set about repairing it. When the Book of the Law was found and read, Josiah tore his clothes and joined in the repentance of his people. God was pleased with the youthful king because "his heart was tender," and when at fifteen years of age Josiah began thirsting after God in a more intense way, what a rich reward was his in his godly reign. If you are a parent or if you have the care of the young, may grace and patience be yours to teach the young at your side to do that which is right in the sight of the Lord.

The Polished Corners of the Temple

"Glistering stones." *1 Chronicles 29:2.*

Among the most valuable things David prepared for the Temple he was not permitted to build were all manner of precious stones. What the exact nature of these costly gems were is not easy to determine. The American Standard Bible gives us "stones of antimonys" for "glistering stones." The Revised Standard Version at Isaiah 54:11 has "stones in antimony" for "thy stones with fair colours." Antimony is a bright, silvery-white, metallic substance used in many ways. Applied to the stones David stored up to adorn the Temple, antimony can suggest their sparkling beauty and splendor.

Smooth and brilliant stones can be made more beautiful by being polished with their own dust. Roughly cut and coarse at first, a diamond for instance, is rubbed and rubbed again with diamond dust and thus made to sparkle. We say that "experience teaches fools." But this proverb is only partially true, for experience also teaches those who are wise. As "living stones" we take on a better polish as we rub against our old sins and mistakes and learn to leave them behind. When we learn from our failures, they become like the dust of our old selves to make our lives "glistering" for him, the brilliant chief cornerstone.

Peter's tears of repentance over his denial washed his heart and gave him a more polished witness for the Master. Peter reminded us that all who come in repentance and faith to Jesus as to "a living stone, rejected by men, but choice and precious in the sight of God" (1 Pet. 2:4) are themselves made "as living stones, built up as a spiritual house" and shine before the Lord in his temple forever and ever. While here below, our heavenly lapidary, the Holy Spirit, is unceasingly active removing all that is coarse and rough in the Lord's jewels, as the redeemed are called. As cornerstones we are being polished after the similitude of a palace or being cut as diamonds to adorn his palace with its gates of pearl.

A Lot of Little Things

"She fastened it with a pin." Judges 16:13–14.

The Bible is the most fascinating Book in the world to those who love and study it under the inspiration of its divine author. For instance, have you noticed that it even speaks about *pins*—little things we often lose more of than use? The three or four references to such appears to indicate a means of fastening. Ezra said, "Give us a pin," words we often repeat if we want to fasten some cloth material together. It must be understood that the pin Delilah used to entangle Samson's hair and the pins of the Tabernacle were not the same kind of article as the common steel pins we can buy so cheaply today. Doubtless, they were made of wood and fashioned more like pegs.

But let us see what lessons a slim, shiny, sharp-pointed pin can teach us. We have a saying, "You could have heard a pin drop," which means it is silent and noiseless in action. Is this not how the Holy Spirit works in heart and mind? Another old expression is, "Bright as a new pin." If a child is clever, he is referred to as being bright. As a child Jesus grew in wisdom, and he will ever remain a shining example to the young.

Further, pins are of little use if they are blunt. To fulfill their function they must be sharp. When Paul wrote, "Diligent in business serving the Lord" (Rom. 12:11) he implied that we must not be dull or blunted in any way. Pins may be a lot of little things, but the smallest pin has both a point and a head—the former being necessary to pierce the torn garment to be repaired, and the latter to prevent its going too far. We speak of one who is a success in life as having "a good head." A pin's head seems to say, "I stop here." Do we not need grace to guide us when to start and when to stop? All who work with pins know only too well that a crooked pin cannot fulfill its purpose. Jesus died and rose again that crooked lives might be made straight and then fit for his use.

What's in a Name?

"Hadassah, that is Esther." *Esther 2:7.*

Although no divine name is found in the Book of Esther, there is no other book in the Bible in which divine providence is more conspicuous. God is shown as overruling in the affairs of his own people in a foreign land. Secretly he works until his purpose is achieved. "Standeth God within the shadows, keeping watch above His own," wrote James R. Lowell.

Esther the orphan girl was brought up by Mordecai, her cousin, who treated her as his own daughter, and she is the central figure of the book bearing her name. What intrigues we see in the double name given the young Jewess by the sacred historian—Hadassah and Esther. Names and their meaning are an absorbing theme.

Hadassah was the original name of this fair and beautiful exile, an interesting name meaning a myrtle. Mordecai took this precious plant into his home long before the Persian king took her into his palace, and nurtured her until she became a lovely plant of renown. Her physical beauty was matched by an inner loveliness of soul. Too often a beautiful face is spoiled by an unholy heart.

But Hadassah's name was changed to *Esther* which means a star. And a star shines forever. Even when she became a great queen, Esther's fear of God and humility shone like a star. The story of Persia's happy queen can be summed up in a sentence, namely, that through God's overruling providence the myrtle became a star. Esther grew up like a *myrtle* and came to glow like a *star.* Her character illustrated the significance of her two names. A myrtle is ever green and cheers the winter as well as the summer. Its leaves also have a sweet fragrance. God would have his myrtles ever fruitful and fragrant. A star sparkles because God clothed it with light. There it shines, "Up above the world so high, like a diamond in the sky." If the true myrtle characteristics are ours, then we shall shine as the stars forever. As myrtles, we too shall become stars.

The Liberal Deviseth Liberal Things

"He giveth more grace." *James 4:6*, RV.

James the Practical, as he has been called, was also a preacher of the generosity of God who, being liberal-hearted, devises liberal things for humankind. "He giveth to *all* men liberally" (1:5). James remembered the word of the Lord Jesus that "whoever hath, to him shall be given, and he shall have more abundance" (Matt. 13:12), and so he wrote, "He giveth more grace," or grace upon grace.

God never limits the supply, nor is he ever weary of giving, though we are of asking and receiving his ever-expanding grace. The width of God's sympathy is seen in that he gives to all. *Whosoever will* may beg at his footstool, for he is most catholic minded. As for his bounty, James described it as liberal. God always gives with an open hand, never meagerly, partially, or grudgingly. He loves a cheerful giver since his is an unmeasured and unmerited grace. If he gives joy, it is always unspeakable.

The magnanimity of God's liberal heart comes out in James' phrase, "God . . . upbraideth not" (1:5). He blesses all who seek his abundance in the gentlest way. "He mingles no acids with His honeycomb. . . . He is too eager for my temporal and spiritual wealth to mar the welcome gift with the harsh word," said an unidentified writer.

Further, James leaves us in no doubt as to the certainty of God's response to what we ask him if we lack, not only wisdom, but other virtues, making us more effective witnesses. It shall be *given him*! From experience James himself knew how liberally God answered prayer. It was said that the apostle's knees were hard as a camel's because of his continual kneeling before God. How encouraging it is to know that we cannot carry to our generous God a petition which dismays or boggles him and that the more we desire, the more he will grant! In 1873 P. P. Bliss wrote a hymn that focused on James 4:6:

> *Have you on the Lord believed?*
> *Still there's more to follow;*
> *Of His grace have you received?*
> *Still there's more to follow.*

Strives in His Little World of Man

"Why dost thou strive against God?" Job 33:13.

The American Standard Bible gives this verse a softer tone: "Why do you complain against Him, That He does not give an account of all His doings?" As he does according to his will which is perfect, why should God give an account to the little world of humankind of what he does? The call is, "Be silent, O all flesh, before the Lord!" (Zech. 2:13). Because he is the omnipotent God, he is not responsible to puny humans who often complains about divine providence. But he is not accountable to any and will not be questioned by the curious or called to an account by the proud and curious.

With our finite minds we cannot fully understand the divine purpose behind many of the perplexing experiences of life, but when we see him face to face, then all will be made clear, and we shall bless the hand that guided and the heart that planned. Because of the perfection of his character, he demands that we trust him where we cannot trace him and be acquiescent on the ground of the promises of his Word. To strive against him or to resist him is actually rebellion and treason, for his designs, although mysterious to us, are always gracious and good, and his ways are all righteous. In his ode to Napoleon Bonaparte, Byron had this verse:

> *'Tis done—but yesterday a King!*
> *And armed with Kings to strive—*
> *And now thou art a nameless thing;*
> *So abject—yet alive!*

Those who continually strive against the King of kings, against his Word, his commands, and some of the dispensations of his providence, become as nameless things and abject. His wisdom is infinite; his love is unchangeable; and his power is unlimited. Therefore, let us not strive against but submit to his perfect will and trust him completely.

For His Bounty—There Was No Winter In't

"God said, Ask what I shall give thee." 1 Kings 3:5.

Actually, God presented Solomon with a blank check to draw what he liked from heaven's never-failing treasury. But the young king took no undue advantage of God's bounty which knows no winter of scarcity. All Solomon desired was "an understanding heart to judge thy people, that I may discern between good and bad" (1 Kings 3:9), and God bountifully supplied Solomon with unusual wisdom so that "there was none like thee before thee, neither after thee shall any arise like unto thee" (1 Kings 3:12). We link God's request, "Ask what I shall give thee," to Christ's word to his own, "Ask, and ye shall receive" (John 16:24), to emphasize that heaven does not respond indiscriminately and give us anything we ask for—"Ye ask and receive not, because ye ask amiss" (Jas. 4:3). Had Solomon asked for long life, riches, or the life of his enemies, he would have asked amiss and not received. Scripture must be balanced by Scripture. John said, "We know that we have the petitions that we desired of him" (1 John 5:15), but he was careful to affirm that God only responds to requests, "If we ask any thing *according to his will*, he heareth us" (1 John 5:14). Therefore, in all the things we ask for, there must be the observance of this proviso—*according to his will.*

God always gives freely and plentifully when there is harmony between his will and our petition. Having boundless resources, he is never straitened in himself and constantly asks us to avail ourselves of all we have in him in whom there dwelleth "all the treasures of wisdom and knowledge" (Col. 2:3). Like Solomon, we can pray for wisdom since our understandings need to be enlightened and our wills brought into perfect harmony with the will of God and our affections fixed on him and on holy and heavenly things. From an unknown source we read:

> *My life, my crown, my heaven, Thou art!*
> *Oh, may I find in Thee my heart.*

Out of Debt, Out of Danger

"Owe nothing to anyone, except the loving one another."
Romans 13:8, Handley Moule.

What a better place this old world of ours would be to live in if only all of us shared the expressed hatred of Charles H. Spurgeon, nineteenth-century preacher, for *dirt*, *debt*, and the *Devil*. In a most congenial way Paul closed his precepts of civil order with the universal command to love. As those forgiven for our spiritual debts we must avoid absolutely the social disloyalty of debt and, with watchful care, pay every creditor in full. How striking is Emerson's phrase, "Pay every debt, as if God wrote the bill!" All who have been redeemed by the blood of Jesus should be prompt and punctual in payments and should not be guilty of rash speculations resulting in heavy debt, which is a breach of the divine precept. They should live within their means and not bring disgrace upon their Christian witness by contracting debts they are unable to pay. Too often, in order to keep up with the Joneses, large debts are incurred that become a burden.

As believers we should be more concerned about adorning the doctrine of God our Savior than about spending money we do not have to keep up appearances. The one debt we are to be deep in is that of love. Said Handley Moule, eighteenth-century English bishop of Durham, "Love is to be a perpetual and inexhaustible debt, not as if repudiated or neglected, but as always due and always paying." And an unknown writer said:

Let those who bear the Christian name their holy vows fulfil;
The saints—the followers of the Lamb—are men of honour still.

97

Like a Living Coal His Heart Was

"Thou shalt heap coals of fire upon his head."
Proverbs 25:21, 22.

How impressive is Longfellow's description of Hiawatha whose:

Heart was hot within him,
Like a living coal his heart was.

Only those whose hearts are warm like living coal can practice the injunction of Solomon and earn divine reward. In ancient times the process of melting and purifying metal was crude. Rough nuggets of gold were hard to soften, and the refiner would not only have fire beneath a crucible but would pile fire all around it and over it until it was buried in fire with heat reaching the metal from beneath, around, and above. Heaping coals of fire on the head of the crucible greatly helped to melt and refine the silver.

The application is not hard to discover. The scribes and Pharisees had broken the divine law regarding love of the brethren and of enemies. Their hearts were not hot with love within them. When Jesus came, he gave the old commandment new life by his wonderful example of loving us, even when we were his enemies. Long patience was his, but he knew that the gold of hard hearts melts slowly. Burying them in the warmth of his love, he heaped coals of fire upon them until his foes were made friends.

The divine way to treat those in need of succor and kindness is to mollify them as the refiner melts his metal in the crucible, not only by putting it over the fire, but by heaping coals of fire upon it. We can transform enemies into friends only by acting toward them in a loving, friendly manner. Nothing can nourish those in need like "the milk of human kindness." The psalmist's heart was strangely warmed by the marvelous kindness God showered upon him in a strange city. When we love our enemies, bless those that curse us, do good to those who hate us, and pray for those who despitefully treat us and persecute us, we heap coals of Calvary's fire upon their hearts and heads.

98

Adversary versus Advocate

"Joshua . . . standing before the angel of the Lord, and
Satan standing at his right hand to resist him."
Zechariah 3:1.

In his most illuminating commentary on Zechariah F. B. Meyer said
that the one thought which pervades the prophecy of Zechariah is
"*Hope*, for he is pre-eminently the Prophet, as Peter is the Apostle, of
Hope." This feature is clearly evident in the chapter before us, taken
up, as it is, with the divine rebuke of Satan. In the opening verses there
is conflict between the adversary and the advocate, with the latter
proving victorious over the former. Some writers suggest that "the
angel of the Lord" is a person of high dignity in the angelic realm; he
may have been Jesus in one of his preincarnation appearances. But
that could hardly be so here in light of Zechariah 1:12, 13, where the
personality of this special angel of the Lord is distinct from the Lord
himself.

Satan, whose name means *adversary*, has been the adversary of
humankind from man's creation. Satan was justly rebuked by the Lord,
for "who shall lay anything to the charge of God's chosen?" The saints
of God are still accused by Satan who ever stands by to resist them as
they seek to live and witness for the Lord. But their source of relief and
victory is the knowledge that Jesus, their mediator and advocate, is
standing by, enabling them to resist all the fiery darts of the satanic
adversary. When assailed by Satan, let this be our constant encouragement that Jesus is standing by our right hand to preserve us against
those who would condemn us. Paul, when heavily assailed by hellish
influences, had no one standing by him, but he could say, "Notwith-
standing, the Lord stood with me, and strengthened me" (2 Tim. 4:17).
Anne Steele of the eighteenth century wrote:

> *Look up, my soul, with cheerful eye,*
> *See where the great Redeemer stands*
> *The glorious Advocate on high.*

99

Clear Shining after Rain

"Not joyous but grievous; nevertheless afterward."
Hebrew 12:11.

The writer of this wonderful Epistle was dealing with God's chastening his redeemed children and also with the results of every pain God permits them to feel. He would have us know that the ripest benefits are sorrow-borne. William Cowper, whose "Olney Hymns" gave us the title of this meditation, also wrote in "Epistle to a Protestant Lady" that:

> *The path of sorrow, and that path alone*
> *Leads to the Land where sorrow is unknown.*

Divine searching and scourging are not joyous but grievous; nevertheless afterward we come to bless the hand that guided and the heart that planned even though part of the plan was pain.

How full of significance is *afterward*! How despairing it would be if there were no *afterward* to explain the meaning of our tears! Scripture is replete with records of saints like Joseph, Hannah, and Job who, severely tried and tested, came to experience a blessed afterward. God's discipline of his redeemed children is never misguided but always wisely administered for their profit. Those who allow themselves to be corrected by it come to prove its beneficial and blessed results. Harsh plowing yields joyful, bountiful harvests.

From an unknown source we learn that the believer "grows rich by his losses, rises by his falls, lives by dying, and becomes full of being emptied." His grievous afflictions result in the peaceable fruit of righteousness in this life and the full vintage of joy in the *afterward* of heaven. There are times when the heart is perplexed over what God may permit in life, but patience must be allowed to do her perfect work. The *cross* may be our lot today, but tomorrow, the *crown*. A hymn writer declared:

> *We may not fully understand*
> *How underneath God's chastening hand*
> *Pain is fulfilling love's command*
> *But afterward!*

100

His Droppings of Warm Tears

"I tell you even weeping, that they are the enemies of the cross of Christ." *Philippians 3:18.*

Those warm Christlike tears of Paul dropped, not only over those who were utterly godless and positively hostile to the idea of a man dying for their sins, but over those who professed Christ and sought shelter beneath his cross. Paul's tears, his liquid agony, over those in the Philippian church indicate at once the tenderness of the mourner and the awfulness and certainty of the coming ruin of those who were enemies of the cross because they did not see in it the evil of sin. They had the horrible belief that although under grace they could give the reins to sin instead of being strangers to its attractions. They would not submit to the authority or confirm themselves to the example of Christ who died upon the cross. To them Christian *liberty*, which Paul preached, meant *license*. Continuing in sin, that grace may abound, those Antinomian Philippians made themselves the enemies of the cross. Having thus "turned the grace of God into lasciviousness" (Jude 4) they earned for themselves the severe judgment of destruction.

If the cross is all our glory, then we must never by conduct or conversation bring disgrace upon it. We must strive in every possible way to advance its victory, spread its glory, and bring sinners to trust him who was crucified upon it for their salvation. Because that wondrous cross is the foundation of our hope, the key opening the gates of paradise, the object of angelic wonder, and the cause of Satan's everlasting destruction, it should give us pain to be considered its enemy in any way.

May grace be ours never to be ashamed *of* the old rugged cross or a shame *to* it. May he who died in our room and stead enable us to glory in his cross, spread its glories, declare its triumphs, and hold it up in the face of a sinful world as its only hope for life, here and hereafter.

Every Fool Will Be Meddling

"He that . . . meddleth . . . is like one that taketh a dog by the ears." *Proverbs 26:17.*

This proverb must be seen in light of the times when Solomon penned it. The Jews, failing to understand that a dog could be trained for useful service, sadly neglected it until it became an unclean animal and a by-word for reproach. To call anyone *a dog* was the greatest insult. Sometimes a few dogs would snarl and quarrel over a morsel of food in the street, and a man would try to seize the most angry dog in the group by the ears and drag it away. But the longer he held the ears, the more exhausted he became, and letting go, he was bitten by the dog.

Solomon makes the point that anyone meddling with strife that has no personal application is likely to be bitten. If the passerby had let the dog alone, its fit of temper would have subsided, and the animal would have left the street in peace.

What a lesson for meddlers! As Solomon goes on to say, only fools meddle with strife not belonging to them and only add fuel to the fire. Further, it is foolish to meddle so as to cause a quarrel, as some misguided folks are fond of doing. If a friend becomes ill-tempered, one should not vex him or her still further. "A soft answer turneth away wrath; but grievous words stir up strife" (Prov. 15:1). It is always unsafe to meddle in other people's affairs if we can do no good. The golden rule for our conduct at all times and under all circumstances was laid down by Jesus: "Whatsoever ye would that men should do to you, do ye even so to them" (Matt. 7:12). It was he who made peace by the blood of his cross and who can enable us to be at peace among ourselves.

Thou Hast Conquered, O Galilean

"A stronger than he shall come upon him." *Luke 11:22.*

In our Lord's discourse about casting out demons there is no doubt that his illustration symbolized his victory over Satan. A strong armed man was guarding his palace and his goods, and a stronger man came and conquered him, taking from him the armor he trusted.

As the stronger, Jesus came upon the boasted strong man and overcame him. Thus, through the life, death, and resurrection of Jesus, Satan is a conquered foe. We sing about marching *on* to victory. Actually, since Calvary, we march *from* victory. Triumph over all satanic foes, as well as the security of our redemption, was in his final cry of conquest, "It is finished" (John 19:30).

Now, by faith, we make his victory our own. Satan still vaunts his strength as the enemy of all righteousness and as the unwearied foe of the saints. We know only too well that he excites to sin, accusing us of sin before God and striving to overcome our faith in God and his Word. But as the result of Calvary's victory over Satan, we can steadfastly and successfully resist him through all that Christ, his grand opponent, is to us.

Satan may be a deadly serpent, but Jesus is the brazen serpent which heals. Satan is still a roaring lion whose roars warn us of his attacks, but Jesus is the prevailing lion of the tribe of Judah. Satan, as a wolf, seeks to harry the little flock, but Jesus is the Good Shepherd and protects his sheep. Satan is ever our foe, but Jesus is our abiding friend. Satan is a liar and the father of lies, but Jesus is the Truth. Satan is branded as the accuser, but Jesus is extolled as the advocate. Satan is portrayed as the prince of darkness, but Jesus is the light of the world and of life. Satan has the evil reputation of being a murderer since the beginning of humankind, but Jesus is the resurrection. Satan boasts his power and position as the god of this world, but Jesus is God over all and is stronger than the world's hellish deity. We sing with A. C. Dixon:

> *Jesus is stronger than Satan and sin, Satan to Jesus must bow;*
> *Therefore I triumph without and within; Jesus saves me now.*

The Household of Continuance

"Evening, and morning, and at noon, will I pray."
Psalm 55:17.

The church of the living God is composed of those who represent the "household of continuance" in the spiritual grace of prayer. Paul, agreeing with the psalmist, said that we must "continue in prayer, and watch in the same with thanksgiving" (Col. 4:2) and "pray without ceasing" (1 Thess. 5:17). Praying at morning, noon, and night implies that prayer must be considered a *habit* or that we should speak to God at all times and in all places whether there are immediate occasions for its exercise or not.

St. Augustine expressed the hope that when Christ appeared for his translation he would find him either praying or preaching. Such continuance in prayer is independent of *place* or *time*. Some are slavishly dependent upon a place, which can become a hindrance to true prayer. An aged minister asked a plain, prayerful servant girl how she would interpret Paul's exhortation about praying continuously. "Can you pray all the time with so many things to do?"

The girl's reply was, "Yes, Sir, the more I have to do, the more I pray. When I awake in the morning, I pray, 'Lord, open the eyes of my understanding.' While I am dressing, I pray that I may be clothed with the robe of righteousness. When I have washed, I ask for the cleansing of the blood. As I begin my work, I pray for strength equal for my day. As I sweep the floors, I pray God to sweep all dirt from my heart with His besom. Then, as I prepare the meals, I ask God to feed with His manna and the sincere milk of the Word. When busy caring for the little children in the house, I ask my heavenly Father to carry me as His child. And so, on through the day, Sir, everything I do furnishes me with a thought for prayer."

The minister was overwhelmed and said, "Well, Mary, you have certainly learned how to pray without ceasing."

Have we? We sing of prayer as the "Christian's vital breath," but is it? If we cease to breathe, physically, we die. Unconsciously we breathe without ceasing and so live. Place and posture in prayer are observed at given times, but to *continue* in prayer means praying at all times and in all places and having one's life itself a *prayer*.

Thought Is the Child of Action

"I will run the way of thy commandment, when thou
shalt enlarge my heart." *Psalm 119:32.*

Benjamin Disraeli gave us the dictum, "Experience is the child of
Thought, and Thought is the child of Action." *Running* implies vigorous
action, but, said David, we must run on the track of the divine Book.
To run and not be weary is dependent upon the enlargement of heart.
The strong action of the heart in all holy things comes as the result of
the Spirit's operation upon it. Only those who wait upon the Lord
can run without weariness.

Our great physician knows that all spiritual disease is heart disease
which must be remedied before there can come effective action in service.
Athletes know that running is a strong, healthy movement of the whole
body, requiring energy and necessitating a sound heart. We cannot run
in the way of God's commandments except in the strength and vigor he
calls "enlargement of heart," which means a love for and cheerfulness
in doing the will of God.

Walking and sitting Christians are more common than *running*
Christians, who make haste and delay not. Paul described the Christian
life as a race which we must all have to run, and run well, if we would
win the prize. When there is enlargement of the heart by God, there is
an outgoing beyond all the limits self-ease would impose. Heartiness as
action for God depends upon the heart cleansed, and kept clean, by
him.

Our hearts must be daily enlarged to take in the ever-growing
thoughts of God. When he fills the heart to the limit, he enlarges its
capacity to receive more, and so the faster we run. We recognize that
walk is often used to denote the habitual obedience of our life in Christ,
but the term *run* signifies the energy of such a life. Scripture also has a
good deal to say about rest, and some hold that this and not action is
the rule and privilege of a Christian's life. But it is neither. The
Christian's privilege is rest for the soul; the Christian's rule must be
action for the energies. Rest is justification in Christ's blood; action is
the power and unction of the Holy Spirit.

None of Self, and All of Thee

"Not I, but Christ." Galatians 2:20.

Paul ever practiced what he preached. Galatians 2:20 is the imperative rule he laid down for himself and for every child of God. This rule smites yet heals, beggars and exalts. It strips the believer of all self-interest and self-glory and then changes emptiness into fullness and defeat into victory. May each of us, with Paul, experience what it is to give Christ the preeminent position in all things.

Theodore Monod in his heart-searching hymn traced the gradual step from *I* to *Christ:* "All of self, and none of Thee"; "Some of self, and some of Thee"; "Less of self, and more of Thee"; "None of self, and all of Thee." And this should be our ruling passion.

The impressive Keswick hymn, bearing the initials A.A.F., exemplifies our text:

> *Not I, but Christ, be honoured, loved, exalted,*
> *Not I, but Christ, be seen be known and heard;*
> *Not I, but Christ, in ev'ry look and action,*
> *Not I, but Christ, in every thought and word.*
>
> *Not I, but Christ, to gentle soothe in sorrow,*
> *Not I, but Christ, to wipe the falling tear;*
> *Not I, but Christ, to lift the weary burden,*
> *Not I, but Christ, to hush away all fear.*
>
> *Christ, only Christ, no idle word e'er falling,*
> *Christ, only Christ, no needless bustling sound;*
> *Christ, only Christ, no self-important bearing,*
> *Christ, only Christ, no trace of I be found.*
>
> *Not I, but Christ, my every need supplying,*
> *Not I, but Christ, my strength and health to be;*
> *Christ, only Christ, for spirit, soul, and body,*
> *Christ, only Christ, live then Thy life in me.*
>
> *Christ, only Christ, ere long will fill my vision,*
> *Glory excelling soon, full soon I'll see;*
> *Christ, only Christ, my every wish fulfilling,*
> *Christ, only Christ, my all in all to be.*

The question of paramount importance is, Does Jesus reign supreme in your life and mine? Count Zinzendorf never tired of saying, "I have only one passion, it is *He!*" Are we consumed by such a passion?

Veni, Veni, Emmanuel!

"They shall call his name Emmanuel, which being
interpreted is, *God with us.*" *Isaiah 7:14; Matthew 8:23.*

Among the prophetic, symbolic names given to Jesus, none is more
expressive of his condescension in being made in the likeness of man
than that of *Emmanuel*. The sign Isaiah gave the people was of goodwill
to Israel and particularly to the House of David which, though its fulfillment would be some five hundred years later, brought much assurance
to the nation that God would not cast it off. A Messiah would come on
a glorious mission, wrapped up in a glorious name—*Emmanuel*, "God
with us!" James Mason Neale's translation of a ninth-century Latin
chant reminds us of Israel's hope:

> *O come, O come, Emmanuel*
> *And ransom captive Israel.*

Matthew opened his Gospel by announcing the supernatural birth of
this heavenly being, "breaking His way to earth through a virgin's
womb in fulfillment of the prophecy that He should be called *Emmanuel*,
or 'God with us.' " Both the names *Jesus* and *Emmanuel* belong to him
who came as the manifestation of God to humankind, as the God-man.
Since *Jesus* means "Jehovah–Savior," both names are freighted with
an implication of the deity of its bearer. Had he not been *Emmanuel*, he
could not have been Jesus the Savior. How comforting is this precious
name Emmanuel! God is our nature; he is with us in our sorrows and
trials, in our lives and service, in our homes, and at the end of the road
translating us to Emmanuel's land above. We sing with John Newton:

> *Sweeter sounds than music knows,*
> *Charm me in Immanuel's name;*
> *All her hopes before my spirit owes,*
> *To His birth, His cross, His shame.*

109

Lessons from a Spider's Web

"The hypocrite's hope shall perish . . . whose trust shall
be a spider's web." *Job 8:13, 14.*

While we are all fascinated as we watch spiders weave their beautiful
webs, we nevertheless think them horrid insects and seek to destroy
them. Yet, in spite of our aversion to spiders, we must not forget that
they only fulfill the instinct which an all-wise Creator implanted within
them and they are of much value to us in diminishing the swarms of
insects by which we are molested. Bereft of these wily hunters, we
should be plagued like the Egyptians of old with flies.

While popular prejudice has always been against the spider, earning
the unknown poet's description that it is "cunning and fierce, mixture
abhorr'd" because of the way it decoys the little fly into its parlor, we
can imitate its prowess in seeking to destroy that which is evil. We all
know about the lesson King Robert the Bruce learned while hiding in a
cave from his foes. He watched as a spider tried again and again to
weave its web.

The spider's skill as a weaver is remarkable, for its web, though frail,
is a marvelous production, distinguished by beauty of design, fineness
of construction, and sensitivity to touch. Alexander Pope's couplet
expresses it:

> *The spider's touch, how exquisitely fine,*
> *Feels at each thread and lives along the line.*

The whole fabric is spun out of its own body and is a part of the spider's
life. Thus it should be with our service for the Master which comes out
of a life utterly given to him. But with all its beauty, wonder, and
design, the spider's web is so easily destroyed. Job made this application when he reminded us that the hypocrite's hope, so cleverly con-
ceived, will perish as a fragile web. His hope is the creation of his own
fancy and therefore doomed.

Threefold Cord of Gospel Truth

"Keep in memory . . . Christ died for our sins . . . thanks be
unto God for the victory." *1 Corinthians 15:2, 3, 57.*

The well-known American novelist, Peter DeVries, in an article "The
Age of Innocence," described how he helped a young Chicago girl to
whom he became attached in his youth. Catechism classes were held in
the basement of the Dutch Reformed church, and Peter helped the
youthful Greta brush up on her lesson so that she could appear to be
sound in doctrine. He posed the question that would be asked of her by
the examiner, "What three things are necessary for thee that thou
mayest live and die happily?"

"*First*, how great are my sins and miseries," she gave the answer.

"*Second*, how may I be . . . let's see . . . Delivered. Delivered from
my sins."

"*Third*, How may I express my gratitude to God for this deliverance?"

Recognition, emancipation, and adoration are the aspects of our faith
we must not forget. We must keep in memory the necessity of the
recognition of our sinful condition before a thrice-holy God and repentance or contrition because of such. The order is "repent" and then
"believe the Gospel." Discovering how great are our sins, we must turn
in penitence and faith to him who died for our sins and experience the
perfect deliverance he made possible from the penalty and thralldom of
those sins. Paul would have us remember that this deliverance is of a
threefold nature: *past, present, perspective* (2 Cor. 1:10). Would that
the multitudes around us fettered by iniquity could experience the
glorious deliverance, the blood of the cross secured! What else can this
blood-bought emancipation result in but adoration. We express our
gratitude to God when, with Paul, we exultingly cry, "Thanks be unto
God for the victory" (1 Cor. 15:57). Such gratitude not only escapes
our lips but is manifested in a life of obedience and devotion to him who
died for our sins. But not until we join the ransomed throng above, who
washed their robes and made them white in the blood of the lamb, shall
we praise, worship, and adore him as he merits.

111

Brothers All in Honor

"This honour have all the saints." *Psalm 149:9.*

All who are saved by divine grace are brothers and sisters in grace and thus share equally in the honor of being a people near unto the Lord and living with the high praises of God in their mouth, and a two-edged sword in their hand. Honor becomes an empty bubble if we do not realize how signally we have been honored of God. When asked to cover the stars on his uniform, Lord Nelson replied, "In honour I gained them, and in honour I will die with them." All we have through grace was gained for us by the honor of our substitute, which has become one eternal honor. This honor, it will be noted, is the possession only of the *saints.*

Who and what is a saint? In the Roman Catholic Church a member must have achieved eminence in some particular way and have been dead for many years before being canonized as a saint. But all God's saints are living and have been redeemed by the blood of his Son, with some being more saintly than others.

Among all the titles given the believers in Scripture, *saint* is the most expressive one of the lives they must live as followers of their holy Lord. "Be ye holy, for I am holy" (1 Pet. 1:16). Called to be saints, what is our honor? It is being born again of incorruptible seed, even of the Word of God by the Spirit, being acknowledged as the sons of God, being closely allied to him who died for our sins, being heirs of God and joint-heirs with Jesus, being forever freed from the slavery of sin to serve our heavenly deliverer in liberty, having him as our representative and advocate on high, knowing that when he appears in glory it will be for our glorification, being appointed to sit with Jesus in the judgment of angels and in his universal reign. Are we confident and conscious of these great privileges and living under their sanctifying influence? Then sing with an unknown hymn writer:

> *Pause, my soul, adore and wonder,*
> *Grace hath put me in the number*
> *of the Saviour's family!*

O Living Waters, Rise within Me Evermore

"Spring up, O well; sing ye unto it." Numbers 21:17.

Although this is the only reference in Scripture to the well of Beor, it became famous because it was the subject and object of a divine promise. God had told Moses to gather the thirst-stricken people to the place and there he would give them water. The remembrance of that provision, and the blessings brought by that spring for the Jews and their cattle, remained green in the memories of the people who fashioned it into strange traditions. As the people slaked their thirst, filled their vessels, and watered their cattle, they burst forth into that song of joy of which we have only a fragment, "Spring up, O well; sing ye unto it."

In a time of revival, when there is a marvelous upspringing of the Holy Spirit's power in the salvation of the lost and the quickening of saints, what holy joy there is. There is an acute spiritual thirst today, and multitudes are dying in sin because of the lack of the water of life. May ours be the sincere, heartfelt prayer, "Spring up, O well."

May the Spirit so possess all preachers of the Word that out of them living waters will flow to those smitten with thirst. As we think of the well of Beor, we are reminded of another hot day, hundreds of years later, when another leader, thirsty and weary, sat by Jacob's well at Sychar and promised a more refreshing water that would spring up into life eternal. We must remember, however, that what God has promised to give we must earnestly inquire after and prepare for. That well of Beor was the object of effort, for we read that "the nobles digged it with their staves" (Num. 21:18). As Charles H. Spurgeon put it:

> The Lord would have us active in obtaining grace. Our staves are ill adapted for digging in the sand, but we must use them to the utmost of our ability. Prayer must not be neglected; the assembling of ourselves together must not be forsaken; ordinances must not be slighted. The Lord will give His grace most plenteously, but not in the way of idleness. Let us, then, bestir ourselves to seek Him in whom are all our fresh springs.

May there spring up that marvelous grace of God in fountains over the whole earth, causing the dry places to blossom as the rose and to be beauteous as the garden of the Lord.

114

The Lamp That Ever Shines

"The commandment is a lamp, and the law is light."
Proverbs 6:23.

Solomon must have had in mind his father's use of the lighted lamp as a simile of Scripture, for David had written, "Thy word is a lamp unto my feet and a light unto my path" (Ps. 119:105). God has hung up in the heavens the lamp of the sun, moon, and stars to pour a flood of light upon the darkness of earth, but a *light* still brighter than the sun and which, like the sun, never goes out, never sets, never requires trimming or relighting like a lamp of our making, is the light of truth in God's holy Word.

Such is the nature of this perpetual, infallible lamp that it gives more than we can use, shines brighter when trial and sorrow make life darkest, and can shed its light through the valley of the shadow of death to the very gate of heaven.

A lamp is of no use if there be no light within it. Thus, if there is any distinction between these two figures of speech, *lamp* and *light*, we can think of the *lamp* as the written Word itself—the Bible, printed and bound up and ready to be read and studied. The *light* is the Holy Spirit within it who inspired holy men of old to fashion the lamp and who ever waits to shed light upon its precepts and promises and enlighten our minds to understand and receive them. "The letter killeth—the Spirit giveth life—and light" (source unknown).

It is comforting to know that we can take this divine lamp and hold it, making it our very own to throw light upon our way as we journey through life. From another unknown source we learn that the Bible is indeed the light of our dark sky:

> *A lantern to our footsteps*
> *Shines on from age to age.*

When the Spirit shines through the lamp, he brings the truth to sight, causing the commandments and counsels to shed a searching light upon our hearts and lives. How right William Cowper was when he wrote that

> *A glory gilds the sacred page,*
> *Majestic, like the sun:*
> *It gives its light to every age;*
> *It gives, but borrows none.*

To Endless Years the Same

"Thou art the same . . . thy years shall have no end."
Psalm 102:27.

The psalmist speaks of God's unchanging, unending years throughout the generations. The earth and the heavens he fashioned have grown old like a garment and have disappeared, but "thou art the same." Since God is the ever-present deity, the division of time into past, present, and future has no relevance to his existence. "From everlasting to everlasting" he is God to whom a thousand years are but a day. We may spend our years as a tale that is told, but as the one without beginning and ending, God has no such tale to tell. Time is broken up for us into years, months, weeks, and days, but to God, from eternity to eternity is one unbroken whole.

Until time shall be no more, our earthly lives will be made up of sections of time. Occasionally, we should pause and take stock to discover whether we have been a profit or a loss to the king himself. Have we come short in holiness, spiritual advancement, faithfulness, and diligence? If so, let us repent and correct the balance and have the king blot out the handwriting against us.

Further, we cannot but be grateful that although "time, like an ever-rolling stream" may have borne dear ones away, God has been gracious in filling the vacant place in heart and home with more of his own abiding presence. What else can we do but raise our Ebenezer and trust in the promise that all God has been he will continue to be in all the future holds for us. "The Lord hath been mindful of us: he will bless us . . . . We will bless the Lord" (Ps. 115:12, 18).